S0-BNJ-032

CLOSE FOR SUCCESS

The Key to Real Estate Sales

CLOSE FOR SUCCESS

The Key to Real Estate Sales

Jim Londay

Dearborn
Financial Publishing, Inc.

While a great deal of care has been taken to provide accurate and current information, the ideas, suggestions, general principals and conclusions presented in this text are subject to local, state and federal laws and regulations, court cases and any revisions of same. The reader is thus urged to consult legal counsel regarding any points of law—this publication should not be used as a substitute for competent legal advice.

Executive Editor: Kathleen A. Welton
Acquisition Editor: Wendy Lochner
Project Editor: Roseann P. Costello
Copy Editor: Toni O'Gorman
Interior Design: Edwin Harris
Cover Design: Salvatore Concialdi

©1988 by Dearborn Financial Publishing, Inc.

Published by Dearborn Financial Publishing, Inc.

All rights reserved. The text of this publication or any part thereof, may not be reproduced in any manner whatsoever without written permission from the publisher.

10 9 8 7 6 5 4 3 2

Library of Congress Cataloging-in-Publication Data
Londay, Jim.
    Close for success.

    Includes index.
    1. Real estate business. I. Title.
HD1375.L658   1988   333.33'068'8   88-6837
ISBN 0-88462-739-X

DEDICATION

For Mary, Sarah, John and Bridget

Contents

Closing is a Series of Small Steps. Rules for Confident Closing.
The Results of Not Closing. Closing with the Authority of an
Expert.

*Buyers Buy Houses Based on Emotions, Not Logic. Every
Property Has a Fair Range of Value. The Closer a Property Is
Priced to Its True Market Value, the Faster It will Sell. The
Houses that Sell the Quickest Usually Sell for the Most. Sellers
and Agents Do Not Decide What the Property Is Worth. Sellers
Determine How Quickly Their Property Sells. If a Property
Does Not Sell, the Price Is Too High. Price Is the Determining*

Factor in How Quickly a Property Sells. There is No Direct Relationship Between Cost and Value. How Incurable Defects Affect Market Value. How Financing Affects Market Value. Prospects Buy Payments, Not Price. The Role of Brokers and Salespeople.

CHAPTER 3   QUEST and HQF   29

The QUEST System. The HQF System: *Chapter Summary.*

CHAPTER 4   Basic Closing Approaches   37

The Foundation Close. The Write-Them-Up Close. The Ask-For-The-Order/Tie-Down Close. The Ben Franklin Close. The Boil-Down Close. The Original Motivation Close. The Reversal Close. The Silent Assumptive Close. The Let's-Get-This-Hammered-Out Close. The Urgency Close. The Give-and-Take Close. The I-Was-Wrong Close. The Split-the-Difference Close. The Final-Point Close.

CHAPTER 5   Closing When Prospecting   47

Prospecting for Sellers. *Obtaining Appointments with Owners of Expired Listings. Obtaining Appointments with For-Sale-By-Owner Prospects. Prospecting Open-House Visitors. Prospecting Future File Candidates. Open-Ended Questions for Sellers. For Owners of For-Sale-By-Owner Properties. For Owners of Expired Listings. For Sellers in General.*

CHAPTER 6   Closing When Listing   55

Answering Objections to FHA/VA Financing. Objections Regarding Commission Rates. Specific Objections and Solutions when Listing. Listing For Sale By Owners. *I'm Going to Save the Commission.*

CHAPTER 7   Earning the Seller's Cooperation   69

Educating the Seller During the Listing Presentation. Chapter Summary.

Preface

In my 16 years in real estate, I have met thousands of real estate salespeople. Many were highly successful. Their ability to close, not a vast store of technical ability or market knowledge, was the basis of their success. Their ability to motivate a buyer or seller to take action was their greatest asset in putting sales together on a daily basis. *Close for Success* was written to teach you the secrets used by the top producers in our industry and to show you how you can incorporate them into your working dialogue.

The essence of selling real estate is helping people solve their real estate problems. Successful salespeople do this by helping their clients and customers make the best decision when buying or selling. You must be comfortable helping clients make major decisions because the average sellers or buyers are incapable of making these decisions when left to their own devices.

Buyers and sellers would have very little need for real estate salespeople if they knew enough about real estate to make informed decisions. Finding the "right house" once the buyers are qualified is relatively easy. Getting the buyers to make the commitment in writing is a challenge. Determining the right price and marketing strategy for a property is relatively easy. Getting sellers to list their house at a saleable price, terms and condition is a real piece of work.

There are no "born" salespeople. Closing is a combination of art and science that has been mastered by thousands of salespeople through dedication and hard work. With honest commitment, you, too, can possess the skills of a true master.

Selling anything, whether it be a product or service, can be broken down into two basic steps. One, finding customers and two, getting them to buy. The customers, whether sellers or buyers, buy your services. The sellers, your clients and customers of your services, buy your ability to market their house to obtain the fastest sale at the highest possible price. The buyers, although not always your clients, not only buy a house, they use your services in helping find the best house for their needs, wants and abilities. In effect, both buyers and sellers are buying your ability to close.

Chapter 1 discusses the basic nature of closing, including principles that can profitably be used in all sales. Chapter 2 explains basic marketing principles buyers and sellers need to know to make an informed decision. Chapters 3 through 14 teach specific closing techniques that may be used in daily customer-salesperson situations when listing and selling real estate. Let's jump in. The water is fine.

Acknowledgments

I received immeasurable assistance in writing this book from the following people: Jill Garnatz, my friend and confidant for her countless hours at the wordprocessor transcribing text, correcting grammar and syntax, and providing me with excellent advice on content and structure. Kathleen Welton, Executive Editor of trade and professional books at Longman Group, and editor who knows how to get things done. Roseann Costello, Project Editor and Toni O'Gorman, Copy Editor.

Thanks also go out to my incomparable wife Mary and my three loving children, Sarah, John and Bridget. Their support will forever be appreciated. Although it is impossible to name them all, I thank each of the salespeople and students over the years who have freely shared their ideas and techniques, many of which are in this book.

Jim Londay

1

The Nature of Closing

Closing is the process of leading a prospect through the stages needed to complete a sale.

Gathering the necessary elements of a transaction and finalizing the duties and obligations is part of that process. Hammering all the parts of a transaction together is truly what the term *closing* means. Closing occurs during the *entire* sales transaction.

It is frequently said that "the best qualifiers are the best closers." The reason for this is simple. Qualifying and closing are the same thing: a series of questions. Common sense tells us effective qualifying and closing dramatically shorten the time it takes to put a sale together. When working with buyers, prequalifying them to determine their needs, wants and abilities before ever showing them a house allows you to do a better job in less time. This is a critically important step that should be thoroughly completed with every buyer and is explained in detail in chapter 3, "QUEST and HQF."

Qualifying your sellers consists of asking enough questions to enable you to advise them on how to sell their property at the highest price in the shortest time with the fewest problems. Steps to accomplish this can also be found in chapter 3 under the section titled "QUEST and HQF."

Selling real estate is a disorganized activity. Imagine yourself in the Houston Astrodome in a weightless atmosphere. There is no set starting or ending time. The transactions occur in a different location every time, and the steps of every sale take a different course in every instance. Floating around in this weightless atmosphere are buyers, sellers, loan packages, loan officers, loan underwriters, appraisers, closing secretaries, other real estate salespeople, termite inspectors and surveyors. Your job is to grab one of each and to keep them all in place while grabbing one of each of the other required elements. While all of this is happening, the elements you already put in place have a tendency to drift unless there is a hand keeping them firmly in place.

This disorganization provides a golden opportunity for individual salespeople and brokers. You may never become the world's expert on converting highrise office buildings to condominiums or developing industrial parks, but you can become the leading expert in one niche in your local marketplace, be it sales of existing houses in your farm area, new home sales, condominium sales, multi-unit brokerage or whatever field you choose.

CLOSING IS A SERIES OF SMALL STEPS

Selling real estate is the largest transaction in most people's lives. The salesperson must break it down into little segments that the buyer or seller is better able to cope with and accept. These little decisions merge together and result in a final decision to sell or buy a property. By obtaining a series of small agreements, you form a workable transaction. The small agreements form the basis for the big decision.

Effective salespeople consistently apply what I call the *Continuous Close Technique.* They treat every situation as a closing situation and are continuously asking questions, applying trial closes, using tie downs and moving the customer toward the desired final decision. By doing this, they formulate the series of small agreements that form the basis of the transaction. A truly great salesperson persistently closes without the customer's awareness. Contrary to common sales lore, closing does not mean taking out a pen to obtain a signature. In fact, the closing process should be nearly or entirely complete by "autograph time." If you wait until "signature time" to try to close, you will usually meet resistance instead of commitment.

Resistance when "writing the order" can be lessened by anticipating and resolving objections before they occur. The major objections of prospects are almost always the same. Sellers rarely want to price their house competitively. They do not want to pay discount points. They want to negotiate the commission and seldom want to make improvements or repairs to help the property sell quickly. Buyers' concerns include location, floor plans, color schemes, schools, churches, financing, required down payment and monthly payments. Effective salespeople persistently search for the objections and concerns most important to their prospects.

Only by tuning into the customers' feelings and motivations can you resolve the road blocks to a sale. This requires developing a "closing sensitivity" to ensure that you are focusing your efforts on the real, not merely the expressed, concerns of your prospect. Buyers and sellers often build "smoke screens" to throw you off the trail. This is frequently unintentional. It is an unconscious defense mechanism prospects use to postpone making a decision. It is your job to see through these smoke screens to determine the real objections and to move the customers ahead. The ability to get to the real objections is necessary to reach a final resolution. The same is true with sellers. When left to their own devices, most sellers do not know how to correctly price their property, put it in prime condition or offer the terms necessary to attract a buyer. Helping people make decisions is the principal reason real estate salespeople exist. Buyers and sellers cannot get the job done without our expert help.

> Our job is to help sell the property at top dollar in the shortest period of time for the seller and find the right house in the right location with the correct financing for the buyer.

RULES FOR CONFIDENT CLOSING

A prospect's level of comfort, or put another way, state of nervousness, is a reflection of the demeanor of the salesperson. To capture and maintain the prospect's respect, the salesperson must maintain authority and close with complete confidence and ease. The following guidelines can help you accomplish this.

1. Be calm, relaxed and confident throughout the entire selling process.
2. Project a "we can make this work" attitude. After all, any problem (closing opportunity) you encounter has been resolved in thousands of instances where circumstances were basically the same.
3. Treat all problems encountered as minor bumps in the road to be resolved. Explain to the customer that the present setback is a minor factor that will have little impact on the overall objective.
4. Adopt the premise that every problem is resolvable. Every problem has one best solution and, through the mutual effort of all parties, the best solution will be achieved.

Developing a "closing sensitivity" requires setting the correct emotional tone for every situation. A closing master instantly and effortlessly demonstrates any of the following characteristics.

Be gentle.   Prospects are often overwhelmed with the size and scope of the decision. Being gentle with the prospects when they are shaky will get them through a minor emotional crisis and set the stage for a decision.

Be inquisitive.   All good salespeople are curious and inquisitive. They are continuously asking open-ended questions to determine their prospects' true wants, needs and abilities.

Be enthusiastic.   An effective salesperson's enthusiasm closely mirrors that of the customers'. If you show potential buyers a house and the buyers say, "This is not what we were looking for at all," you tell the buyers, "Yes, I am somewhat disappointed myself. This is not at all like the listing salesperson described." If you go to the next house and the buyers say, "Say, this is kind of nice," you also are going to like the house. As they are more excited, you will get more excited. When the buyers like the house, your level of enthusiasm should be slightly ahead of theirs. This encourages the buyers to become emotionally attached to the property. Save your enthusiasm for the houses that most interest your buyers. If you are excited about every house, your enthusiasm will lose its meaning.

Be strong.   Remember most houses are bought and sold on emotion and not logic. Prospects may become upset or angry, even hostile sometimes. When they do, you need to be strong. Do not get trapped in an emotional argument with your customers. Remain calm, cool and proficient, and you will be able to keep sales together that the average salesperson would lose.

This does not mean you bottle up your emotions. On the contrary, I want you to control your emotions and display them on demand, when it is the right time for you to be exasperated, upset or demanding to most effectively close.

Be humorous/Be serious.   At different times and with different prospects, you can be humorous or serious. A humorous comment will frequently break the tension, relax the customers and bring them to the right frame of mind for procuring a signature. With other prospects, reaching an agreement is a solemn, "no joking" experience. With these people, be "all business" and treat the transaction more as a nuts and bolts affair.

Be analytical.   Some prospects insist on weighing all the pros and cons. They need to feel they have taken all factors into consideration. Be analytical with these people. Go through every aspect of the transaction and intertwine their emotions with the logical reasons why they should make the commitment.

Be aloof.   Some prospects respond to aloofness. You are in the "right house" and they are quite excited about it while you are somewhat aloof. This is sometimes referred to as the "negative sell," where the customer thinks you are a buffoon because you obviously cannot see that this house best meets their wants. You can do some expert closing here.

Be an expert/Display leadership. Many people do not have enough knowledge about buying or selling real estate to make an intelligent decision. They cannot make the decision without "expert advice." You are that expert. Unless you can carry an air of power, knowledge and competency, you are never going to be the ultimate closer.

Be disappointed. Sometimes the absolute best close is to be disappointed. "Dan and Susan, we have looked at a number of houses, and you have agreed this house best meets your needs and abilities. After all the work we have done, I am somewhat disappointed you are not ready to make a decision."

Be authoritative. Some people are incapable of getting anything accomplished without direction and outside help. They need someone to tell them when to do it, how to do it and in what order. If you have these types of prospects, take charge and lead them through the steps.

Be understanding. "I understand how you feel" are five of the most powerful words in a salesperson's vocabulary. No matter how silly a statement prospects make, no matter how utterly wrong they are in their assumptions, no matter how wrongheaded their statements, you can always say, "I understand how you feel" or "I understand how you feel, but have you ever considered this aspect?" or "I understand how you feel, but have you ever looked at it from this angle?" or "I understand why you feel that way, but there are other possible solutions."

Lack understanding. "Tom and Cindy, this contract accomplishes everything we set out to do when we originally put this house on the market. I do not understand your reluctance in accepting this offer."

The above described emotions are to be blended seamlessly into the ongoing process of making real estate sales work. As mentioned earlier, you do not express these emotions because you feel them. You call upon them when it is the right time in the decision-making process to produce the results you want.

THE RESULTS OF NOT CLOSING

The results of not closing cost not only you, but also your buyers and sellers in the following ways.

Failing to close with sellers produces expired listings. It is as simple as that. When sellers hire you to sell their house, they do not list it with the thought that ten months later they will still have an unsold house and no prospects. They list it with the thought that it is going to be sold and closed within a reasonable period of time. To get the house sold, and this is an ironic aspect of the real estate business, we have to get the sellers to do a series of things they do not want to do. We need them to price the property correctly, which they are reluctant to do. We need them to offer competitive terms, which they frequently resist. We need them to put the property in a good saleable condition, which they are often hesitant to do without our encouragement. Getting the sellers to do all of these things is a form of closing. If we fail to close in this way, we have cost our sellers a timely sale at the top of the fair price range. This produces monetary losses for the sellers in two ways: reduced sales net and increased costs due to unnecessary extra payments caused by a delayed sale.

"But my sellers do not like it when I ask them to do these things." And I do not like it when the dentist tells me I need a tooth filled. But I do it because the dentist is the professional I hired to do the job. The patient does not decide if his or her tooth needs to be filled. Sellers should not decide how their property should be marketed. That is why they hired us.

It is usually impossible to produce a sale and have the sellers enjoy doing what it takes to sell the property. That is not the way it works. Sellers hire us to produce results, not to be their friend. Being their friend is nice, but the best way to be friends with customers is to deliver the results they hired you to produce.

Another way to lose when closing with sellers is by failing to effectively and promptly close on good offers. This often means losing a buyer through that deadly "let's go back and forth" routine. Contract presentation time is not a time for game playing because the buyer will frequently walk.

A third and particularly dismaying time to lose a sale through a failure to close is when you have a sale put together that falls apart during the pending period. Failing to close in this situation means failing to put that sale back together time and time again until it is closed. The mark of an expert in this business is the ability to take problem sales, get the sellers and buyers to accept a solution, no matter how painful, and get it closed.

I conducted a recent seminar on presenting offers and went through the series of closes outlined in chapter 12. After the seminar, one of the attendees came up to me and said, "I was that seller." I asked him what he meant. He said, "I was that seller. I had a salesperson just like you who went through close after close after close until I accepted the contract. At the time, I did not think accepting the contract was the best thing to do, but upon closing the sale and seeing houses similar to mine sit on the market for another eight to ten months, I could not have been more thrilled that I had been closed on by a real expert." That particular seller realized after the fact that closing ends the pain and uncertainty all sellers feel when marketing their house.

The cost of not closing can be equally high for buyers. Failing to get the buyers to submit an offer when the correct property is found frequently results in them losing the one house that best fits their needs and abilities. There are few situations in real estate that are more disappointing than having good buying prospects lose the house they wanted because they needed a little more help in making the decision than the salesperson was able to give. That little extra close that could have meant the difference between them living in their dream house and then having to settle for second best was neglected.

Another risk you run in failing to close promptly with buyers is the risk of increasing interest rates. In the real estate business, rates are either going up or down. Recent years have seen increased volatility in the size and frequency of rate changes. Failure to get a prompt decision commonly ends with the buyers having to pay additional loan fees or higher interest rates. If they have found the right house and they qualify under the current rates, the time to close is now, not later. After all, when interest rates are low, only three things will normally occur: (1) rates will go up, (2) prices will go up or (3) both will occur.

CLOSING WITH THE AUTHORITY OF AN EXPERT

A student of mine, new to the business, approached me with a problem. She had a listing she could not sell. She asked me if I would take a look at the house and give her my opinion of what the problem was in exchange for buying lunch. I excel at lunch and, of course, I agreed. I toured the house. The condition was excellent and the offering terms were competitive. That left price as the only possible problem.

After going through the house, she said, "Well, why hasn't it sold?" "The price is too high," I responded. She asked, "How much too high?" I said, "Somewhere between five and ten percent. Get the price knocked down and it will sell because it looks great and the terms are favorable. She made an appointment with her sellers, went in with complete confidence and told them the problem was the price. She obtained an adjustment and sold the house.

This encounter perplexed me, because in the course she took, I stressed the fact that if a house does not sell it is either price, terms or condition. If the condition and terms are okay, it *has* to be the price. She had heard my rallying cry on this point dozens of times. How could she have missed it so completely? I finally figured it out. She was relatively new in the business, having been selling real estate for only about three months. She lacked the total self-assurance and self-confidence that comes with experience. Although on an intellectual level she knew the price was the problem, on a gut-instinct level, she was not sure and she needed the reassurance of an "expert" to tell her this was the problem before she had the self-confidence necessary to convince her sellers. This book was written to teach you how to play the role of an expert with your buyers and sellers that I played with this salesperson. You have to be able to go in and tell your buyers and sellers with absolute confidence what course of action they should follow. Unless you truly believe in your own advice, they will not believe it and certainly will not follow it.

If you want to buy me lunch to go through the house with you as this salesperson did, I will accept. But ask yourself this: How much of an expert can be bought for a $14 lunch? Save the $14, have faith in your own conclusions and forge ahead.

2

Educating the Prospect

Selling real estate differs from other types of selling in that we rarely have to create a need. In most cases, we are working with buyers whose needs are immediate. Otherwise, we should not be working with them. Likewise, we should only list properties of sellers who are motivated and desirous of an immediate sale. Selling most products or services, be it life insurance or lawn care, requires creating a need. The fact that real estate salespeople are not required to create a need makes selling real estate more of an educational process than a "selling" process. If we educate our prospects as to how things work, they are more likely to make the decision that is in their best interest much sooner than they would otherwise.

Every person resents being told "You do not need an explanation, just do it this way." I resent that, and most everyone else does also. Good salespeople avoid this type of confrontation by explaining the reasons why buyers and sellers should take a recommended course of action.

Sellers are more likely to list their house at a saleable price, terms and condition if you take the time to educate them as to how the marketplace works before listing their property. If you explain to buyers all the steps they will go through from qualifying to closing the sale and taking possession, they, too, will be much more likely to work in a cooperative way in finding the right property in the shortest amount of time.

The following are basic marketing principles that apply to real estate. Understanding these principles is the first step in increasing your effectiveness with prospects. The second step is to develop dialogue that can be used to teach these principles to the buyers and sellers with whom you work.

Buyers Buy Houses Based on Emotion, Not Logic

People like to think they bought their home using good, business-like, logical reasoning. In virtually every case, this is not true. Most people look at houses until they find one they fall in love with and then come up with dozens of logical reasons why that house is better for them than all of the other thousands of houses on the market. In most cases, buying a personal residence is much more of an emotional decision than it is a logical decision. The sellers' best chance of selling their house at the top of the fair range is to turn the buyers on, get them emotionally attached and get them to fall in love with the property.

Appeal to the buyers' emotions when marketing properties. Sell the benefits. Buyers are not merely buying shelter. When they buy their personal residence, it is an extension of themselves. It is a statement to the world that says "This is who I am," a reflection of their personality. Although you need to carefully qualify buyers as to their abilities, wants and needs, it is imperative that you understand that their decision on buying the house will be based on the emotions tied to those wants and needs.

Every Property Has a Fair Range of Value

In most neighborhoods, there is an approximate ten percent range between the highest and lowest selling prices of similar properties, with most of the similiar properties selling right in the middle of that ten percent fair range. The top of the ten percent fair range is the sellers' price. That is the price the sellers want because it is the highest price at which the property can reasonably be sold. The bottom of the ten percent fair range is the buyers' price because that is the least they can expect to pay to buy that type of a house in that neighborhood. When we list a house, our job is to sell it at the top of the fair range. As discussed in the above section, the best way to do this is to get the buyers to fall in love with that property and think they cannot live without it.

To get the buyers to fall in love with the property and sell it at the top of the ten percent fair range, the property must be in immaculate condition, the sellers must offer financing terms competitive with similar houses on the market, and the property must be priced close enough to its true market value to generate showing traffic and a purchase offer. This brings us to our next basic marketing principle.

The Closer a Property Is Priced to Its True Market Value, the Faster It Will Sell

To illustrate this point, I explain to my sellers "The tale of ten houses." Imagine there are ten properties listed in the same subdivision. They are all of the same style and square footage, and they would all look the same in the multiple-listing book. One of the ten houses is priced at $82,000. Eight of the properties are priced between $83,000 and $89,000. One property is priced at $95,000.

Those of us who have been in the business for some time know what the person who has listed at $95,000 is going to say. "I am ready to deal, but I have to see an OFFER. Why don't they make an OFFER? I would be ready to make some kind of adjustment if I could just see an OFFER." I have known many good salespeople, but I have never met one who could sell a house without the buyers looking at it. We cannot produce an offer on these properties because we cannot get anyone to look at the house. Prospective buyers do not look at every house on the market. They probably will not look at all ten of these listed houses

in one subdivision. Experience and common sense tells us virtually all of the prospective buyers will look at the property priced
at $82,000. We also know that in all probability not one buyer
will look at the property priced at $95,000. It is basic "Marketing
101" that the closer a property is priced to its true market value,
the quicker it will sell. By consistently using the tale of ten
houses, you can get your sellers to see the folly of overpricing
their property (see table 2.1).

The Houses that Sell the Quickest Usually Sell for the Most

It only makes sense. The reasons that make a house sell for the
most money—great location, wonderful condition, competitive
financing terms and a price that will generate showings—are also
the same reasons that make a property sell quickly. The best time
to sell a single-family dwelling is in the first six weeks it is for sale.
Generally speaking, a significant adjustment will be required to
sell the property if it is not sold in the first six weeks on the market. A frequently heard lament is "Well, if I could have waited
longer, I am sure I would have been able to get more money."
That is very possibly true, but when sellers list their property,
they do not list it with the thought of receiving their net proceeds
ten months down the road. Most sellers want to sell their property, close the sale and receive their proceeds check within three
to four months. To do that, we need to generate a sale within six
to ten weeks. Holding the property an extra six months to sell it
for an extra two or three thousand dollars is senseless. The extra
payments of principle, interest, taxes, insurance, utilities and
maintenance will more than offset any increase in the final net
obtained by holding out for a few extra thousand dollars.

An additional problem is that a property will become stale
the longer it stays on the market. When a property is first listed,
the listing salesperson and the fellow salespeople in the salesperson's office are excited and will try very hard to sell that property.
The longer the property is on the market, the more likely it will
be looked upon by the listing salesperson and other salespeople

---

TABLE 2.1   The Tale of Ten Houses

When looking at the information in the multiple-listing book, all ten of these properties appear the same regarding general location, style, square footage and condition. They are priced as follows:

One property is priced at	$82,000
Eight properties are priced between	$83,000–$89,000
One property is priced at	$95,000

Questions:
If you were a buyer, which of these properties would you be most likely to look at? Which one would you probably not look at, at all?

The tale of these ten houses tells us that the closer an owner prices a property to its true market value, the more showings will occur and the quicker the property will sell.

---

as a loser. The staler a property becomes in the eyes of real estate salespeople and prospective buyers, the less likely the property will sell anywhere near the top of the ten percent fair range.

Sellers and Agents Do Not Decide What the Property Is Worth

This is, of course, true. If it were not, all properties would sell for much more than they actually do. Many sellers will say, "I am not taking a penny less than $125,000. If the offer is less than $125,000, don't bring it by. If I cannot get $125,000, I am going to keep it forever." Property owners have this right. However, this does not make the property worth $125,000. Sellers are often under the mistaken impression that we can sell a property at *their* price, which we cannot do unless it also happens to be its true market value. We can only sell a property for what it is worth to a buyer. It is a plain fact that a property is worth only what an active buyer in the marketplace will pay for it today, and nothing more.

Another favorite phrase of sellers is "I sold it for less than it is worth." There is no way that this happened. They sold it for what it was worth on that day. Real estate appraisers understand the following principle that most sellers and many real estate salespeople do not.

Any sale of real estate that is an arm's-length transaction determines that property's value on that day. What the buyer pays for it and what the seller sells it for on that day is the true market value of that property.

I have had many real estate salespeople tell me, "I have this property listed and I know it is priced right, but I cannot sell it." I tell them, "No, the price is too high." They say, "Why?" I say, "It has been on the market for any length of time and no one has bought it." That salesperson can show me 15 final sales to justify the sales price. They can come up with reams of market data supporting their price, but unless a buyer can be produced, it is not worth what they are asking if it has been on the market for three months. When calculating the true net received from a sale, do not neglect the costs of holding a property month after month. The sellers' *true* net is the size of their proceeds check *minus* the extra payments, utilities and maintenance incurred during a needlessly extended marketing period.

Sellers Determine How Quickly Their Property Sells

Sellers frequently think real estate salespeople have a magic wand they can wave to produce a buyer who will pay more than the property is reasonably worth. They will then take that same magic wand, wave it and produce a full-price appraisal. This same magic wand is used to get an unqualified buyer approved for a loan. This is absurd. The day I am writing this approximately 50 houses will be listed in the multiple-listing service of which I am a member. Approximately two-thirds of these houses will be sold and closed within four-and-one-half to five months. Approximately one-fourth of them will still be on the market six to seven months from today. They will all be listed with reputable companies and will be in the multiple-listing service. They will be advertised, open houses will be held and an honest effort will be made by the listing salespeople to get the property sold as quickly as possible. Why will some of them close and sell within a reasonable time, while others are still on the market six months down the road? In most cases, the difference was not the real estate company or the listing salesperson. The difference was the price, the offered terms and the condition of the property when it was put on the market. Those three things, price, terms and condition, determine how fast the property sells, not some magical effort or special advertising used by a real estate salesperson or broker. If we really did have direct control over how fast these properties sold, they would all sell in a week. To be an effective listing salesperson, you need to explain to the sellers that advertising is not usually what sells real estate. Correct price, terms and condition are.

Some sellers respond by saying, "Then what difference does it make with whom I list my property?" It makes a difference because by working with the correct listing salesperson, one who understands how the marketplace works and knows how to work with buyers, the sellers are more likely to market their property correctly. Indirectly, salespeople do influence how quickly property sells. If we are good at educating our sellers as to how the marketplace works and good at getting them to market the property correctly, we will have done our job in getting the property sold at the highest price in the shortest possible time. We not only can make a difference, *we are the difference.*

If a Property Does Not Sell, the Price Is Too High

What about the terms? What about the condition? What about the location? People who ask these questions do not understand that price (value) is made up of condition, terms and location. These three factors are all a function of price. You can emphasize the original statement by saying, "If a property does not sell, based on its condition, location and offering terms, the price is too high." Stating it this way may make it more understandable to your prospect.

I once had a builder take one of my real estate classes who said I was all wrong on this principle. He had built a house and put $138,000 in labor, materials and lot costs. The house had been on the market for a year and a half. He was down to an asking price of $124,000. He angrily asked, "Are you trying to tell me that this house is not worth $124,000, even though I have $138,000 in it? You have not even seen the house."

I informed him that I had not even been in the subdivision and that did not make any difference. Proof is in performance. Having been on the market 18 months while continually cutting the price and not being able to generate an offer is proof positive that this property was not worth what the builder was asking, let alone what it cost to build.

I am distressed by the number of real estate salespeople who tell their sellers they just cannot figure out why the sellers' property has not sold. I have to ask what these people are doing in the real estate business. As mentioned, there are only four reasons it does not sell. Location, condition, terms and price. You cannot do anything about location. If location is a problem, it must be reflected in the price. A real estate salesperson on the first day in the business should be able to tell if a property has condition problems, and the salesperson does not have to be in the business very long before being able to detect if the sellers are offering competitive terms. If it is not condition and it is not terms, it has to be price. There is no excuse for real estate salespeople to ever tell the sellers they do not know why their house did not sell.

Price Is the Biggest Determining Factor in How Quickly a Property Sells

Without correct pricing, we cannot generate showing traffic. Without the correct price, we cannot generate offers. Price is the kingpin in determining how quickly real estate sells.

I recently did a study of all residential sales in a section of our metropolitan area. It produced the following results:

- Three out of five properties sold within three percent of the listed price;
- Four out of five properties sold within five percent of the listed price;
- Only three percent of the sales had more than ten percent negotiation.

The results of this show that in my marketplace, if your properties are overpriced by more than five percent, you have very little chance of producing a buyer, no matter what techniques you use. Properties overpriced by more than ten percent, and many are, have almost no hope of selling without an adjustment. Sellers are more likely to price their property correctly once they understand the relationship between listing and sales prices in their marketplace. Spending 45 minutes analyzing market data for your marketplace will give you percentage guidelines you can quote to your customers.

There Is No Direct Relationship Between Cost and Value

Existing properties.   One of the most misguided actions property owners can do is try to determine the present value of their property by starting with what they paid for it some time in the past and factoring in an inflation figure. Typically, they look up some dubious source stating how much real estate has gone up each year for the last number of years, add these percentages together, and multiply them against what they paid for their property, coming up with a mythical figure for a present value. This may occupy some of their time in an amusing way, but it will not tell them their property's present worth. Appraisers of residential property rarely consider final sales more than six months old. That is how quickly the marketplace changes. This, coupled with the wide variations of changes in values of real estate over a city, state or nationwide area, eliminates the possibility of a property having any direct relationship to any type of index.

There are phases in the real estate cycle where a person can buy a property at the top of the fair range and three or four years later discover it is not worth any more than they paid for it, at times less. When I list a property, I do not want to know what the property owner paid for it in the past, because I do not want it to influence my estimate of the present market value.

Occasionally your sellers will say, "My property has to be worth more than what you say it is worth because I paid that much for it three years ago." What they paid for it three years ago does not have a thing to do with what it is worth today. What they paid for it one week ago does not mean it is worth that today. If a buyer purchased a house for $176,000 a week ago, that proves that one week ago the property was worth $176,000. It proves there was a seller willing to sell and a buyer willing to give up $176,000 to possess it. The buyer may have been the only person walking the face of the earth willing to pay $176,000 for that property. There is no guarantee that that property can sell for $176,000 today. Property owners often find this fact distressing, but it is a true function of the marketplace.

New construction.   It is also true in new construction that there is no direct relationship between cost and value. As in the case of the builder mentioned earlier in this chapter, a builder who erects a house on speculation on occasion will end up having to sell it at a net loss. This is frequently caused by the location of the new house.

Appraisers refer to increases or decreases in value due to the value of the surrounding properties as *progression* or *regression*. Progression states that the house is worth more if it is built in a neighborhood of more expensive houses. The principle of regression states that your house is worth less if it is built in an area of less expensive houses. The following examples illustrate this. Imagine a builder constructing two identical houses that would typically sell for $120,000. One of these houses is built in a $160,000 neighborhood. The other is built in an $80,000 neighborhood.

The house in the $160,000 neighborhood could very possibly be worth $135,000 or even $140,000. Conversely, if he built the same $120,000 house in an $80,000 neighborhood, it is unlikely it will sell for even $100,000. As we stated earlier, location is one of the four factors in determining how fast a house sells. Even though once a house is built we cannot do anything about it, location still remains and always will be the largest contributing factor in determining the true market value of a property.

Cosmetic improvements.   Generally speaking, cosmetic improvements add more to the value of a property than they cost to do. I use what I call the *one-in-four rule*.

For every dollar in cosmetic improvements a property needs, there is generally a corresponding drop in market value of at least four dollars.

For example, take a property needing $1,000 worth of paint and carpeting. The dining room, hall and kitchen need to be painted. The living room, dining room and hall need to be recarpeted. The carpet is worn, outdated and dirty. An astute homeowner should be able to paint three rooms and a hall and put down that much carpeting for $1,000. A decision to market the house in its current condition will frequently force the homeowners to sell the property for a discount of up to $4,000, or even more, than what they could have received had they replaced the paint and carpeting. The reason is simple. We go back to the fact that people buy properties based on emotion. In a moderately priced house we will often have first-time or relatively inexperienced homebuyers. They will not look past the fact that $1,000 spent on carpeting and paint will really spiff this house up, and they can get a very good buy on the house. By putting in the paint and carpet, we increase our chances of getting the buyers to purchase the property using their hearts and emotions rather than using logical reasoning. If someone does buy this house before the improvements are in, it is likely to be an investor or an experienced buyer, who make their decisions with their head and not their heart, enabling them to buy it for less.

Refusing to make cosmetic repairs results in a lower price in another way. If the sellers delay in making these cosmetic repairs, they frequently turn off potential buyers the first few months their property is on the market. They use up their self-allotted marketing time, put themselves in a bind and have to slash the price, even if they do make the repairs in order to generate a sale in a reasonable amount of time.

Bringing and keeping the cosmetics up to peak condition is the best investment a home seller can make. In today's marketplace, most buyers want to buy a house that is in "move-in" condition. They do not want to have to paint, clean carpets, replace carpets or vinyl or cut down overgrown bushes and shrubs before they move in. If they have to do these things to buy the house they want, they will sharply discount the price they will pay.

Structural improvements. In most cases, structural improvements do not add as much to the market value of a property as they cost to install. As an example, let's take an $80,000 house that is in an $80,000 neighborhood. The homeowners have decided that the house is too small. They say to themselves, "It is a hassle to move. Payments on a bigger house are going to be high, the kids know the neighbors' kids here and they like going to this school. Let's do a room addition!"

What these property owners do not consider is the following: (1) Moving is a hassle for a week or two. Putting a room addition on your house is a major disruption for three to four months. (2) It is true, payments on a bigger house are going to be quite a bit more. What they do not take into consideration is that their present first mortgage and a short-term, high-interest-rate second mortgage for the room addition will together frequently be more than what the house payment would be if they moved into a more expensive property. (3) The contention that a move creates a serious problem in a child's life has little validity. I have handled the sales of countless incoming and outgoing transferees and have found that it is really not the children who have trouble adjusting. In fact, four hours after they move in, they usually know every kid on the block and are outside playing baseball. It is generally the parents who have more trouble adjusting than the children.

Let's say that the owners do not take these factors into consideration, and they decide to put a room addition on their house. The $80,000 house is built with what an appraiser would call average construction. Typically, the owners build the room addition with what an appraiser would classify excellent construction, with a full-wall brick fireplace, a $1,200 wood sliding door, a wet bar and a huge deck. Depending on locale, the room addition can easily cost the homeowners $25,000. These properties often go on the market within two or three years after the room addition was completed.

At times, the owner is disgusted with the house because of the hassle and inconvenience of adding the room addition. Some realize their unhappiness was not due to a small house, and, of course, we have a normal number of outgoing transferees and people who have had a change in their economic condition and decide they really cannot afford that first and second mortgage payments every month. Naturally, these people want anywhere from $105,000 to $115,000 for their property. The appraisal principle of regression will keep that from happening. This is a $105,000 house in an $80,000 neighborhood. These property owners are often lucky to get half of the cost of their improvement back.

The amount of value added by structural improvements varies widely from area to area. However, structural improvements such as room additions, finished basements, large decks, completely redone kitchens and bathrooms infrequently bring as much in added value as they cost to install. If unsure what structural improvements add to value in your area, ask an experienced residential appraiser active in your area.

Repairs.   Repairs do not add value to a property. They bring the property back up to the optimum market value. All buyers expect a roof that does not leak, a furnace that works and toilets that flush. A property must be mechanically and structurally sound if a sale is expected at the top going price for these types of properties. Buyers will not overlook neglected repairs, and, if they do make an offer, they will make a corresponding reduction at least equal to, and usually more than, it would take to do the repairs themselves.

How Incurable Defects Affect Market Value

Incurable defects are location problems or problems with the site such as steep lots, relatively inaccessible location or structural problems with the property that are so extensive it does not make economic sense to complete them. There are two remedies for these types of problems. One is to reduce the price. The other is to offer extraordinary financing.

Some properties are listed with incurable defects so severe it is unlikely prospects will be buying them for their personal residence's. This leaves selling the property to investors as the only option. If you can make the numbers work, you can find an investor to buy almost any property. Investors in physically or locationally distressed properties are usually most interested in cash flow. The right combination of price and terms will frequently overcome incurable defects that cannot be solved in any other way.

As is true with repairs, buyers will not overlook significant, incurable defects of any type and will reflect that in what they will pay for a property.

How Financing Affects Market Value

To sell a property at the top of the fair range, a seller must offer terms competitive with similar properties on the market. For example, you list a moderately priced property in the $70,000 range. By researching the marketplace for ten or 15 minutes, you determine that two-thirds of the similar properties that have sold in that area in the last six months have sold with FHA or VA financing. The sellers are going to have to offer FHA or VA new finance terms if they are to sell the property at or near the top of the fair range.

Prospects Buy Payments, Not Price

When you think about it, most buyers really do not care what the purchase price of the property is. Their real concern is how much the monthly payment is going to be. If you can find a way to reduce the payments, you can frequently increase the sales price of the property. This was illustrated in a dramatic way when mortgage interest rates went from nine percent in 1979 to $17^{1}/_{2}$ percent in 1982. In many areas of the country in 1982, properties that had assumable FHA and VA loans were selling for a premium of ten percent and more over market value. Properties for sale with nonassumable loans frequently could not sell for what the market data showed to be their worth. These owners not only had to sell at a discounted price, they often had to resort to seller-assisted financing, where they bought down the buyers' loan or carried back some or all of their proceeds in the form of payments. This further reduced their true net proceeds from the sale.

An innovation spurred by the mortgage crunch of the early 1980s was a state-sponsored, tax-free mortgage bond for low-

and moderate-income families. The availability of these funds produced two immediate effects. First, property owners of moderately valued properties who did not have assumable financing were suddenly able to sell their houses in a very short period of time. Second, they were able to sell their houses for far more than they would have been able to had this tax-assisted financing not become available.

The workings of the marketplace during these crisis times in residential sales graphically proved that financing truly is a function of price and net. Use these examples to illustrate this principle to your sellers.

The Role of Brokers and Salespeople

It is the job of all licensees involved to do everything reasonably possible to sell the property for the highest net in the shortest time possible. To do this, we must get the sellers to agree to do things before and during the marketing period they originally had no intention of doing. I have yet to meet the sellers who had a burning desire to pay discount points, yet I have had many sellers who had to pay discount points to get their property sold. I never had sellers who just could not wait to put in new or clean their present carpeting, make repairs and paint their house in order to sell it, but I have had many sellers who needed to do these things to effect a reasonable sale. I have met very few sellers who wanted to price their property at its true value. However, the closer we can get a property priced to its true value, the quicker it will sell.

The pressure from all sources when listing a house is to list it for more than it is worth. Sellers want the highest net possible. I understand that, and I know that this is my job. However, this wish to get the highest net possible encourages sellers to price their property at more than it is worth. You, the listing salesperson, are working in your sellers' best interests, and you want to get them the highest net possible. Sometimes you may try to sell the property for more than it is worth because you like your sellers and you work for them. Another factor is that salespeople often fear losing the listing to another salesperson who has no qualms about "buying the listing." All of these reasons tend to push initial asking prices higher than they should be.

There is no real pressure on the seller or the salesperson to list the property for less than it is worth. Because of this, there is very little chance that a property will be underpriced. However, there is pressure from every side encouraging an unrealistic high price. The basic job of a listing salesperson is to get the seller to list the house at a price that will allow the salesperson to produce showing traffic and a reasonable offer. Increase your chances of doing this by making sure your sellers have a good working knowledge of the marketing principles contained in this chapter.

Basic Real Estate Marketing Principles

People Buy Houses Based on Emotion, not Logic

Every parcel of real estate has a fair range of value of approximately ten percent.

The closer a property is priced to its true market value, the quicker it will sell. Often, properties that sell the quickest also sell for the highest prices.

Sellers and agents do not decide what the seller's property is worth. It is worth only as much as a buyer currently active in the marketplace will pay for it.

Although sellers do not determine what their property is worth, they ultimately decide how quickly it sells by what they price it at, the condition they have it in, and the financing terms they offer.

If a property doesn't sell, the marketplace is saying that based on location, condition and offering terms, the price is too high.

There is No Direct Relationship between Cost and Market Value

This is true in new construction, the sale of existing homes, and when determining how much improvements add to the value of real estate.

How Condition and Improvements Affect Market Value

Properties in top condition sell the fastest in all types of markets, strong or soft.

To receive the maximum profit in the shortest possible time, a seller should have the property in as close to perfect cosmetic condition as possible.

Market value is based on a properties present condition. Buyers rarely pay for potential.

Jim Londay's one in four rule: For every dollar in cosmetic repairs a property needs, there is a corresponding drop in market value of approximately four dollars.

Structural improvements to a property do not usually raise the market value of a property as much as the improvements cost to install. In many cases, a homeowner will receive only 30 percent to 50 percent of the cost of the structural improvements in the form of a higher sales price when the property is sold. At times, not that much.

How Curable and Incurable Defects Affect Property Values

Curable defects (paint, carpet, vinyl, almost all needed maintenance and repairs) reduce market value. You can either correct the defect or reduce the price. In most cases, you must reduce the price more than it would cost to repair the defect to effect a sale.

Incurable defects (location, certain design problems, steep or unusual lots, and some serious condition problems) also reduce market value. They have two possible remedies: reduce the price or offer extraordinary financing to compensate.

Buyers will not overlook significant defects of any type and will reflect that fact when they determine what they will pay for a property. Also, in most cases, they deduct more from what they will offer for the property than the defect would cost to repair.

Basic Marketing Principles *(concluded)*

Financing is a Powerful Tool

To sell their property at the top of the fair range, a seller must offer financing terms competitive with those offered by owners of competing properties on the market.

Prospects buy payments, not price. If a seller can offer a form of financing that will lower payments for a buyer, they will in most cases be able to sell their property for more, and usually more quickly.

Attractive financing can frequently overcome incurable location, design, or condition problems and produce a sale that would otherwise not happen.

The Role of Brokers and Salespeople

It is the job of all licensees involved to do everything reasonably possible to sell the property for the highest net and in the shortest time possible. To do this, we must frequently get the seller to agree to do things before and during the marketing period that they originally have no intention of doing.

3

QUEST and HQF

This chapter provides you with a logical approach to use when working with buyers (QUEST) and a system (HQF) that will help you gain the cooperation of sellers.

THE QUEST SYSTEM

QUEST stands for *Qualify, Understand, Educate, Support* and *Transact*.

Qualify. Qualifying buyers before choosing what house they are to see is the most critical step in laying the foundation of a smooth transaction. Determining wants, needs and abilities is essential to finding the right house in the shortest time possible. The only way we can determine these factors is to ask questions, lots of questions, and completely hear the prospects out. One hour of careful qualifying can save dozens of hours in the field.

I prefer to start the qualifying process by first determining needs. Needs are different for every buying prospect you work

with. Some homebuyers need a house close to special educational ·
facilities for their children. Some have a strong preference regarding a certain church parish or synagogue. Some buyers need a
barrier-free ranch-style house. Others may have received a major
job promotion and now need an executive-level home in which to
entertain. Needs are as varied as the people who buy houses. Determining needs is the first step in narrowing the properties a
buyer should look at.

Once you understand the prospects' basic needs, explore their
wants. In many cases, the wants exceed the buyers' ability to pay.
Wants are a wish list. Early in the qualification process, buyers
should realize that with rare exception—buying a house is a series
of compromises—and they should be prepared to make compromises from their want list. Probe in a patient and tactful manner
to learn as much as possible about the buyers' wants and needs
before qualifying for abilities. Forty-five minutes to an hour is the
minimum amount of time you will need to spend with customers
to determine their needs and wants in a property.

Qualifying for abilities gets more complicated as more differ-
ing and complicated types of loans are introduced in the home-
lending market. At one time, there was only one FHA and one
VA loan program available. There were relatively few conventional loans available, almost all with fixed rates. It was quite
easy to qualify a buyer. In five or ten minutes you could determine with a simple ratio formula how much money they could
borrow. Today, the financing market for houses is far more com-
plex. It is important to have a good working knowledge of what
types of financing are available, but there are now so many financing options available that if a salesperson spent the time necessary to know about every loan available and its qualification
rules, there would be little time left to sell real estate.

The amount of time spent qualifying for abilities varies with
the prospects' available funds, income and job history. At times,
the qualification process is easy. If the buyers have $25,000 and
want to assume a loan and keep the payments below $800, quali-
fying for abilities is complete. However, if the buyers' wants and
needs exceed their abilities, it is often best to rely on the help of a
loan officer. Loan officers are best qualified to counsel buyers on

what type of financing is best for their particular situation and to calculate the maximum loan amount for their current income and liability situation. Your course of action will depend on the complexity of the buyers' finances. At times, the loan officer can qualify the buyers on the phone. Other times, it is beneficial to have your buyers meet with the loan officer in person and spend the time necessary to determine the optimum financing before showing any houses.

This sounds like a large investment of time before showing the first house, but for every hour you spend carefully qualifying your buyers, you will save endless hours in the showing phase. Only by careful qualification of needs, wants and abilities can we narrow the possibilities as far as what houses, neighborhoods and price ranges fit the buyers' interests.

A fellow real estate salesperson approached me after being in the business for two months and told me she had made her first sale. I congratulated her, after which she said it was a particularly tough sale. I asked why it was so hard. She informed me that she took the buyer out 11 times and showed 44 houses. Then she said, "You have an odd look on your face." I said, "I probably do." The salesperson said, "Why, what went wrong?" I said, "Except for out-of-town buyers, it should not take 11 excursions and 44 showings to sell a buyer a house. The only way that could happen if you were working with truly motivated buyers was to start showing houses before you qualified them for wants, needs and abilities. If you had qualified those buyers correctly, there probably would not have been 44 houses to show them."

Understand.   To successfully prepare your buyers for what they will encounter when purchasing a house, we need to understand what the prospects know, where they have been and where they currently are. Are they first-time buyers? Have they bought a number of parcels of real estate? What do they know about actually buying a house? Let's take two examples. You have a corporate executive who is an incoming transferee. He and his wife have moved seven times in the last 20 years. These prospects have considerable practical experience in buying and selling real estate. As our second example, let's take a young couple in their early twenties. The husband is a teacher, the wife is a nurse and they have three children. Their wants and needs exceed what their paycheck can deliver. As first-time buyers, they know very little about the house-buying process. Now that we understand where these people have been and what they know, we are ready to move to the next step.

Educate.   Real estate buyers and sellers are like most of us. They appreciate it when a new proposal is explained in full before they are asked to do anything. By taking enough time to educate our buyers and sellers as to how things work and what to expect, we pave the way for a smooth transaction. Not preparing our prospects for what is to come is not only rude and inconsiderate, it is unrealistic to expect our buyers and sellers to sign a legal document when we shove it under their noses and say, "Just trust me, this is the right thing to do." That "old school" approach is poor salesmanship and will not cut it in today's market.

Let's consider educating our corporate transferee. This is relatively easy. We need to explain to these prospects what areas or subdivisions have the type of financing they are looking for and the price ranges and the type of financing available for that type of housing. Give a few basics about how earnest deposits and purchase agreements are handled in your area, and you are ready to show houses.

Our young couple will need more attention than this. Even though considerable time has been spent qualifying them, additional time should be spent preparing them for what to expect during their house-buying journey. The entire house-buying process should be explained in detail. Discuss agency relationships, who you represent, and what legal rights the buyers have in the transaction. Include why and how they were qualified and how you will pick out what properties to see. Yes, you should be the one to pick out the properties. After all, you are the expert. You are familiar with what is on the market. You are the person best prepared to match their wants, needs and abilities with what is currently available in your market. Explain the entire showing process and what they should be looking for, the contract-writing process and the fact that they will have to come up with an earnest deposit at that time. Prepare them for the size of that earnest deposit, explain how within days they will have a loan application and will have to write yet another check for an appraisal and credit check and possibly a loan application fee. Describe the loan approval and underwriting processes. Explain local "walkthrough" procedures and how early or late occupancies are handled in your location. Finish by describing what they will need to bring to the closing and how that will take place.

Educating your prospects is easy and takes little time. It calms your buyers' nerves and makes it easier for them to move from one stage of the buying process to the next. If you do not prepare your buyers for what is coming up, you are setting them up to be nervous wrecks. You will have on your hands exactly what you have earned and deserve, an anxious and difficult-to-work-with buyer. Take the time necessary to educate your first-time buyers as to what to expect when making a home purchase. It will pay big dividends.

Support.　Although many factors are considered, when it comes down to it, buying a personal residence is usually a decision based on emotional considerations and not principally on logic. Because of this, it only makes sense that we must provide buyers with continued emotional support. They need to be assured they are doing the right thing. Part of selling real estate is being a lifestyle and financial counselor. The support you give your buyers in this role as a counselor will help them in actually making the decision when the time comes.

Transact.　How much care was taken in the first four steps of QUEST will determine how smoothly the final sale is put into effect. The salesperson who spends the time required to qualify the buying prospects' needs, wants and abilities, educates them as to what is going to happen and gives them emotional support throughout, will find putting the transaction together relatively easy. There is a direct relationship between how much time is spent on the *Q U E* and *S* of *QUEST* and how much time it takes to tack the *T* on the end.

QUEST allows the buyers and salesperson to find the "right house" as quickly as possible—allowing the salesperson to do one's real job—getting the buyers to make a major decision they are incapable of making on their own.

THE HQF SYSTEM

HQF stands for the three main concerns of most sellers. *H* for *Highest* possible net proceeds. *Q* for the *Quickest* sale possible. *F* for *Fewest* problems possible.

When used correctly, "The HQF System" will put you and your sellers on the same fast track to success in getting the job done. HQF recognizes that the sellers' motivations and needs are different from those of buyers'. The big job with sellers is not to help them make a big decision, as it is with buyers. By the time we have our first contact with sellers, they have already made the big decision: "We are selling." Although the major decision has been made, there are a number of smaller decisions that must be made in their efforts to attain HQF.

A more direct approach than used with buyers will serve you well when working with sellers. Sellers are not usually looking for a friend, empathy and/or emotional support, which is what many buyers are looking for when deciding which house to buy. What the sellers are looking for can be summed in one word: *Results*. Your entire approach and demeanor should be tilted toward producing the results your sellers are looking for. The sellers' equivalent of qualifying the buyers for needs, wants and abilities is to explain "The HQF System."

The first major point I like to make with sellers is how I view our relationship. In my eyes, the sellers are the employers. I am the employee. I am hired to do the following: Get them as much money as I can, as soon as I can, while handling the problems. Everything I do, everything I give them, everything I counsel them on and all the efforts I make are aimed to produce that one basic goal.

Keeping your focus on the three main concerns of your sellers will make them more likely to cooperate in your efforts to produce a satisfactory sale.

This approach keeps your sellers on track. Sellers have a tendency to focus on trivial aspects of the transaction. When this happens, get them back on track by discussing the important actions that need to be taken when working toward the HQF.

The seller education process.   A large part of achieving success with sellers, as it is with buyers, is educating them as to how the system works. It can range from a half-hour counseling session, where your sellers see the need to try a different marketing approach, to a monthlong effort to educate your sellers as to the true market value of their property. This is covered in greater detail in chapters 6 and 7.

Chapter Summary

Being able to both list and sell is critical to your overall success as a real estate salesperson. Keep in mind that the basic motivations of buyers and sellers are different and that they require different basic approaches. *Apply the QUEST and HQF systems when working with your prospects to keep them and yourself on track.*

4

Basic Closing Approaches

Mastering and matching these basic closing techniques with their complementary situations will dramatically increase your percentage of successful closes.

THE FOUNDATION CLOSE

The foundation close should be continuously used in all situations. Confucius said: "A journey of a thousand miles starts with one step." A $100,000 sale starts with one small *yes*. Moving your prospects step by step toward the final commitment is the surest way to a fast, clean transaction. Build and expand on your buyers' or sellers' comments, establishing agreements and concessions along the way. It will often eliminate last-minute objections before they occur, enabling the smoothest close possible. Dave Stone refers to this as "building a bridge to agreement."

THE WRITE-THEM-UP CLOSE

This excellent close consists of producing a blank purchase agreement and proceeding to fill it in as the buyers give you details. An effective way to help buyers overcome the fear of the purchase agreement is to let them see it early and often. Whenever they mention a pertinent point regarding how they want a sale structured, have a purchase agreement close at hand to fill in what they have told you. If they ask what you are doing, tell them that when the time comes to write an agreement, you want to make sure you include everything they have mentioned, and this is your way of ensuring you do not forget. When they are ready to make a purchase agreement, you can pull out your practice form and a fresh purchase agreement and quickly fill it out.

If your buyers are not ready, this technique will bring out their real objections and provide the opportunity to apply the correct closing technique to get the commitment.

A modified version of "The Write-Them-Up Close" is used when listing a house. At the end of your listing presentation, produce a listing agreement that is completely filled out except for price and possession. This enables you to use "The Write-Them-Up Close" by saying, "We agreed upon $89,950, didn't we, Dan and Susan? The final point we need to discuss is the possession. May I suggest this?" Starting your listing presentation with a completely blank listing agreement can create a cumbersome situation. Make it easy for your sellers to list the house at the end of your listing presentation. "Your approval on this will allow me to go to work selling your property immediately."

THE ASK-FOR-THE-ORDER/TIE-DOWN CLOSE

Perhaps the oldest and most effective closing technique consists of asking the customers if they are ready to make a commitment. Although it is often effective to simply ask, "Joe and Mary Fran, are you ready to buy this house?", it is usually more effective to include a tie down at the end of the phrase, such as "Joe and Mary Fran, I believe it is time to write an offer, don't you?"

"The Ask-for-the-Order/Tie-Down Close" can be used with sellers in this way: "Frank and Betty, I believe we should place it on the market at $149,900, don't you?"

THE BEN FRANKLIN CLOSE

Old Ben gets credit for this one. When it was time for a major decision, Ben would take a plain sheet of paper and draw a line down the middle. On one side he would list the benefits and drawbacks of choice A, on the other side the benefits and drawbacks of choice B. Making the list frequently made the correct decision obvious. It forced Ben to impartially weigh the benefits, problems and solutions. Many salespeople find this effective when the time is right for a decision, but the prospects need a final push to put the commitment in writing.

THE BOIL-DOWN CLOSE

"The Boil-Down Close" is effective when your prospect stalls and continues to come up with bogus excuses. Cutting through these "smoke screen" objections is essential if we are ever going to get the job done. Try something like the following: "Mr. Jones, the fact that the back yard is terraced is a factor in considering buying a home, but I sense it really is not your main concern. Is the fact that your payments will increase from $750 a month to $1,100 a month with this purchase your real concern?

With this type of prospect, you need to keep probing and pushing to find the real stumbling block. Until you confront and resolve these issues, your prospect will jerk you around like a dog on a chain.

THE ORIGINAL MOTIVATION CLOSE

This close is effective when you obtain a contract that meets all of the sellers' original motivations or when you find a house for the buyers that fulfills all of their expressed wants and needs. This close often provides the final push needed to get the buyers or sellers to make the commitment. One example of this approach is to direct the conversation as follows: "Dan and Susan, I sense you are having difficulty making a final decision. On occasion, reviewing your original goals and motivations and how this house (contract) matches and fulfills those goals is helpful." If working with buyers, proceed to show how this property meets, fulfills and resolves all of their original wants and needs in purchasing a house. With your sellers, show them how their acceptance will allow them to finalize their plans to move.

THE REVERSAL CLOSE

This close entails having your prospects reverse positions with the people on the other side of the negotiations.

When your buyers have found the correct house or what you believe to be the correct house and they want to make a ridiculously low offer, use the following approach: "Jim and Mary, you have looked at a number of houses, you have researched the marketplace, you have seen what houses are selling for. Now let me ask you a question. If you were the sellers of this house, would you even consider an offer of $76,000? I do not believe so. Place yourself in the sellers' position. How would you feel if you received an offer of $76,000? You may even consider it insulting." The buyers would have destroyed their bargaining position. "This house best fits the needs and wants you expressed when we originally got together and discussed buying a house. I would hate to see you lose this house by making a ridiculous offer and alienating the sellers."

"The Reversal Close" also works well with sellers. You presented a good offer, but your sellers want to squeeze some blood out of the stone. The close consists of saying, "Joan and Dave, I understand your desire in wanting to counter this offer and get more money out of your house. However, we cannot get more for this house than a buyer is willing to pay. In front of us we have the current market data, which includes final sales, pending sales, expireds and on the markets. We are not the only people with this data. The buyers have access to this data also. In fact, the buyers have been out looking at houses for some time now and they may actually have a better grip on what is available for their money than you do. Ask yourself honestly, if you were the buyers, would you pay more than $84,000 for this house if you had access to this data? I do not think you would. I would like you to strongly consider accepting this agreement." This is often a good time to apply the original motivation or silent assumptive closes.

THE SILENT ASSUMPTIVE CLOSE

This close differs from "The Write-Them-Up Close" in that this is not used until you are completely ready for a signature. Once you have completed your presentation and answered all of the prospects' questions, take the document that needs to be signed, fill in the acceptance portion, sign where the witness is supposed to sign, mark the x's, turn the paper around, set the pen down for them to sign and do not say a word—*not one word*. A prospect cannot and will not pick up the pen and sign if you are speaking. Be quiet. The prospects have two alternatives. They can pick up the pen and sign the agreement or they can raise an objection. If you have done your job correctly, they are out of objections. However, if there is an objection they did not raise and you were unable to detect, this close will often bring the real reason to light.

THE LET'S-GET-THIS-HAMMERED-OUT CLOSE

This close is used late at night after some tough negotiations. You have gone back and forth between the buyers and sellers numerous times. You started out quite a distance apart and are getting close. You are probably as close as you would have liked to have been when the negotiations started, but that was not possible. It is now one o'clock in the morning and one of the parties says, "Gee whiz, it is getting late. Why don't we call it a night and pick this up tomorrow morning?" You say, "No, I do not think that is wise." Experience shows that if you go to bed with only a few minor differences to resolve, the next morning you'll find you are again eight miles apart. "John and Sophie, if you truly want to buy (sell) this house, it is in our best interest to risk losing one more hour of sleep, get this thing hammered out and know that we have a binding agreement and pending transaction."

THE URGENCY CLOSE

"The Urgency Close" can be used with buyers of existing homes and frequently with the buyers of a new home. This close is used after your prospects have found the house that is right for them.

If they delay making a decision, this very house may be sold to someone else from under their feet. This close is most effective when you can relate a true story about previous buying prospects who stalled and were unable to buy the house they truly wanted. "Gary and Diane, I understand this is a big decision, but this particular house fits your financing. It is in the right school district and church parish, the floor plan fits your living needs and the down payment and monthly payments are exactly what you originally expressed. I would hate to see you lose this house by delaying your decision when you know in your heart this is the correct one. Let's move forward on this right now."

Interest rates and financing options provide another variation of "The Urgency Close." "Gary and Diane, interest rates have been skittish recently. Tim Wallach at First Federal has promised that if we can put a sale together, he will hold these interest rates and costs at this quoted amount until noon tomorrow. He cannot extend it beyond noon tomorrow. It would be wise for us to move ahead as a change of only one-half percent interest can mean about $60 a month difference in your payments."

When working with sellers, "The Urgency Close" takes a different strategy. We receive an offer. The sellers are reluctant to immediately respond to the offer and make a commitment. Sellers: "We want to think about it. Can't we sleep on it tonight?" Of course, the answer is *no*. Purchase agreements for residential properties are typically written with a short, almost immediate deadline for presentation. "Joe and Linette, I understand you feel pressured and forced into making a quick decision. That is natural in this situation. Unfortunately, we have until nine o'clock this evening to provide a response for the buyers. If we do not give them an answer, it is the same as writing 'Rejection' across the front with a felt-tipped pen. I am sure you do not want to reject this offer outright, but unless we can formulate an answer to the offer here and now, that is exactly what you will be doing."

Another urgency close that can be used with buyers is the "Buyers Are on Pins and Needles" approach. "Fred and Sally, I understand that responding to this offer in the time we have to consider it is asking a lot of you. Think about the buyers. At this very minute, they are nervous and anxious. It takes a lot to get buyers to make an offer. It does not take much to scare those buyers away by delaying an acceptance or making an unwise counter-offer. Our original goal was to sell this house at an acceptable price, terms and possession. My advice is to quit stalling and get a response down on paper. We need to get back to these buyers as quickly as possible."

THE GIVE-AND-TAKE CLOSE

"The Give-and-Take Close" entails giving up something that is unimportant to your client, but is important to the other party in order to obtain a critical concession.

Sellers' situation: "Bob and Sarah, I understand you do not want to replace the family-room carpeting. It is a significant expense. This contract calls for a closing and possession by May 15. Keeping possession until June 1 is important to you. The buyers have indicated that they can live in their mother's basement for a couple of weeks if possession is critical. Can we effect a trade here where we get the possession extended for 15 days in return for your putting in new carpeting in the family room? The cost saved by not having to live in a motel for 15 days and storing your furniture will more than offset the cost of this carpeting. This is an effective compromise. Let's approach the buyers."

Buyers' situation: "John and Bridget, our sellers are reluctant to pay the discount points you have requested, but have indicated they will pick up the entire cost of the points if you pay $1,000 over the listed price. I understand $1,000 looks like a lot of money, but at today's interest rates, $1,000 is only $8.56 on your monthly payment, and it is not even that when you consider the tax benefits. In return for obtaining this FHA or VA loan, I strongly suggest you consider paying the extra $1,000 in the sales price."

THE I-WAS-WRONG CLOSE

This is used whenever new information comes to light that will cause you to change advice previously given to a client.

Sellers' situation: You failed at your listing presentation because the sellers are convinced their property is worth more than you do. They cause you to doubt the validity of your research. You decide to dig further for more comparable sales and find market data that justifies a somewhat higher price. Immediately call the sellers and arrange for another appointment. Tell them you have uncovered two recent sales that would support a higher asking price for their property than you originally suggested. I do not advocate buying listings, i.e., taking listings that are vastly overpriced with no hope of selling, but I also know that we are all human and, on occasion, make mistakes. When this happens, correct the mistake, go back, get the listing and put a sale together.

Buyers' situation: "I have some really good news for you, Fred and Elaine. I explained your situation to Wendell Jones at First Federal. He suggested some alternate financing that is rarely used, but that can be tailored to fit your exact needs. I was wrong when I told you we could not get you into a house priced higher than $75,000. With this loan program, we can consider going up to $80,000."

THE SPLIT-THE-DIFFERENCE CLOSE

"Let's split the difference." You can split the difference into infinity and never reach an agreement. The "Split-the-Difference Close" can be used effectively, but *only* if the parties are equidistant from a reasonable settlement. Say the property is listed for $130,000. A price of $125,000 is a fair and reasonable market value based on recent solds. You get an offer for $120,000. This is a perfect candidate for the "Split-the-Difference Close" and is far superior to going back and forth in $1,000 increments.

The "Split-the-Difference Close" is not recommended when the buyers and sellers are close. When it comes to small amounts, splitting the difference can alienate one of the parties and spoil negotiations. If you are that close, get an "as is" acceptance and slam it closed.

THE FINAL-POINT CLOSE

This is used when you know the prospect is close to making a decision but keeps rephrasing the same objection. This is generally one of the finest closing opportunities you are ever going to have. Phrase it like this: "Dennis, is the lack of a garage-door opener the only thing keeping you from making a decision? [Don't laugh, house decisions are often made on such minute details.] If we can resolve this issue, are you ready to go ahead?" If Dennis states this is the only thing keeping him from making a decision, write up the sale contingent upon the seller agreeing to install a garage-door opener and get the signature.

5

Closing When Prospecting

PROSPECTING FOR SELLERS

A frequently heard objection when trying to get that first appointment with sellers is: "We're not ready. We don't need a market analysis since we are not ready to sell." They are nervous at the thought of having a salesperson come over, even though they would benefit by the visit. Many sellers believe you are going to strong-arm them into listing their house before they are ready to sell, make them sell it for less than it is worth and take away their proceeds as your commission. This kind of thinking is an obstacle we frequently have to overcome.

A common variation of this objection goes as follows: "You are wasting your time at this point. I don't even know if I am going to sell." They are trying to put you off in a nice manner. The following is an effective response: "Mr. Dubois, I understand your concern. Please let me explain my profession and how I view it. My job is a 'people job,' not a real estate job. It is a people job, where we use real estate to solve people's needs. If I can give you advice, answer a real estate question or help you in any way, my time will not be wasted, even if I don't earn an immediate commission. You may ask, why is this guy so willing to help solve my real estate problems if I'm not ready to list and may not list with him any way? That is a valid question. Seventeen years in the real estate business has taught me that we are selling a service as much as a product. In an area with a strong multiple-listing service like mine, a salesperson can sell any house. The better service I give my prospects, the more business I receive through referrals. Even if you decide not to list or sell your house, or if you decide to sell it For Sale By Owner, or even if you decide to work with another agent, if I do a good job for you here and now, the chances are good you may send me a referral in the future. More than 50 percent of my business comes from referrals generated by helping people with their real estate needs, just like I would like to help you. Any information I give you may prove valuable when you do make a decision, and, of course, there is no cost or obligation. I would like to stop by this week if possible or arrange a time next weekend. Which is better for you?"

Situation: You have called the owners of an expired listing and determined that the owners have not relisted with the old company or listed the property with a new company but are still interested in selling. At this point, they do not think much of real estate salespeople and feel we are all as incompetent as their last salesperson.

They have obviously had a bad experience. Start the qualifying and closing process by asking why their house did not sell. It is important you remain quiet and hear them out. Allow them to vent all of their frustrations. They will rarely mention the real reason the house did not sell. They are rarely going to say, "The house was just overpriced for the location, condition and terms we are offering." More likely, it will be objections such as the following: interest rates are too high, there was not enough advertising, they did not hold enough open houses, we listed with too big of a company or we listed with too small of a company.

Build on their comments by asking for their opinions. "How many open houses did you have?" "What kind of responses did you get?" "How important do you feel open houses are in marketing your property?" Build on whatever they tell you. Once their frustrations and hostility are vented, you can make significant progress toward a closing.

Obtaining Appointments with Owners of Expired Listings

When trying to obtain the initial appointment with the owners of an expired listing, you may hear, "I do not want you to come out. I have decided to take it off the market until next spring." These owners often consider this alternative because they feel the property is not saleable at the time. Try the following approach: "Mr. Sanchez, are you taking your house off the market until spring because you feel it is unsaleable at this time?" If the answer is affirmative, suggest you stop by to take a look at the house, using dialogue something like this: "Mr. Sanchez, every property is saleable if marketed the correct way. Your house did not sell in today's market due to incorrect marketing. I would like to have 45 minutes of your time, so I may look at your house, review what has been done to sell it and explain why it has not sold. I think you will find this helpful, even if you do not place your house back on the market at this time.

"I would like to visit with you this afternoon or this evening, Mr. Sanchez, and go over what we have discussed. This visit will help you determine whether it is better for you to market your house now or wait until spring. I will respect and understand your decision. There is no cost for my visit with you and no obligation on your part other than the time we will visit this afternoon or this evening. Would four o'clock this afternoon or 8:30 this evening work better for you, Mr. Sanchez?" When used correctly, this offer will almost always get you inside.

Obtaining Appointments with For-Sale-By-Owner Prospects

Many For Sale By Owners are reluctant to give a salesperson an appointment to prepare and present a market analysis. The best way to overcome this objection is to offer advice and assistance at no cost and no obligation. Try this approach:

"Joe and Lucy, I understand your desire to sell your house yourself. I would like to help you in that endeavor. There are two things I will do at no cost or obligation that will make it easier for you to sell your property on your own. First, I will prepare a complete market analysis of your house. This will inform you of its approximate value and what you would net from a sale at that price. You can show this to a potential buyer to justify your asking price. The second thing I will do is, if and when you do find a buyer, arrange to have the sale written up by a competent, reasonably priced real estate attorney. I will also arrange for the closing to be prepared and conducted by a title or escrow company, and I can give you the names and numbers of other professionals you will need to call on to complete the sale.

"Why am I willing to do this? First, most FSBOs eventually seek professional help in marketing their property. At this time, you have no intention of listing your property. I understand that, and all I ask in return is to have the opportunity to sit down with you and present how I would market your house. Second, my entire real estate career is built largely on referrals from people I have helped in the past. My willingness to help you at no cost and no obligation is a good-faith effort on my part to earn business in the future. I want you to call me at any time you have a question or need my assistance."

Your chances of obtaining an appointment are increased by making frequent in-person visits with the sellers, each time leaving helpful material you feel they can use to sell their house. These can include qualification forms for different types of loans, explanations of how discount points work (see Example 5.A), current rate quote sheets from loan companies, brochures telling them how to prepare their house for sale, explanations of how a release of liability works on FHA and VA sales and other forms they are likely to need if they are lucky enough to find a buyer. This builds loyalty, increasing your chances of getting the listing, and helps them realize there is far more to selling a parcel of real estate than sticking an ad in the paper, a sign in the yard and having someone fill in the blanks on an agreement. (See *List for Success* for additional information on working with FSBOs.)

Example 5.A

HOW DISCOUNT POINTS WORK

VA guaranteed loans have a maximum interest rate set by the Veterans Administration. This rate is periodically changed to reflect market conditions. They are normally adjusted so they are somewhat below prevailing conventional mortgage rates.

To make up the difference between the maximum VA rate and the prevailing conventional rates, the loan companies charge what are called discount points. One point is equal to one percent of the new loan balance. These points are charged to and paid for by the seller on VA loans.

There is no maximum rate on FHA loans, however, there are still discount points paid in most cases. They are negotiable, meaning they can be paid by the seller or buyer. Frequently, through negotiation, the seller is asked to pay the points on FHA loans simply because the buyers don't have the money. Buyers are not allowed to add the cost of discount points to their new loan.

No seller wants to pay discount points. However, studies have shown that houses sold with FHA or VA financing in which the sellers pay points consistently sell for higher prices than properties sold using other types of financing. Although the seller is charged with this expense on the settlement sheet, in reality, the buyer is paying for most, if not all, of the cost of the points in the form of a higher selling price.

This is substantiated by a study conducted by the Center for Applied Urban Research, a branch of the University of Nebraska at Omaha. The study found that 96 percent of the cost of FHA discount points are returned to the seller in the form of higher selling prices, while 80 percent of the cost of VA points were returned to sellers through higher prices.

Discount point studies have also been conducted in Columbus, Ohio, and Lubbock, Texas. While the three studies came up with slightly different percentages, they all came to the same conclusion: The majority of discount points are paid by buyers through higher selling prices.

Prospecting Open-House Visitors

When initially meeting open-house visitors, introduce yourself and wait for them to do the same. If they do not give you their names, do not press them at that time. Immediately start a conversation by saying, "May I ask you a question?" When you have their permission, begin defining their wants and needs. These should be open-ended questions such as: How big of a house are you looking for? Do you have a specific neighborhood or subdivision you want to be in? Have you discussed the size of payments you would be comfortable with? What floor plan or style of housing do you prefer? Do you have any special needs as far as school districts, church parishes or proximity to bus lines?

As they become more comfortable, ask more in-depth questions, the most important pertaining to their current status: Where do you live now? Do you rent? If you rent, how long of a lease obligation do you have? Do you own? If they own, have they had a market analysis? Is their home listed? If it is listed, has a buyer been found? If a sale is pending, when do you expect it to close? When do you need to give up possession? These questions should be introduced gradually to minimize the prospects' anxiety. As in all sales situations, the person asking the questions, whether it be the salesperson or the prospect, is in control. When directing the conversation by asking the questions, hear your prospect out completely. The more you listen, the more you learn.

If your open-house visitors own their own home and it has not been listed, it is time to start selling the benefits of a market analysis. Stress that the knowledge they will obtain will help them make more informed buying and selling decisions. Explain that the market analysis will include all pertinent data: properties similar to theirs that have recently sold, houses that are currently pending and not yet closed, information on expired listings in their neighborhood and a complete list of all properties currently for sale. Let them know you will include information such as average time on the market, average amount of negotiation, types of financing used in different price ranges and areas of the city, and the success ratio of sellers in their particular marketplace.

If your open-house visitors currently rent or if their current house is already in the process of being sold, you need to determine again their position. Offer your help and stress that there is no cost or obligation in your qualifying assistance. Discuss the importance of a thorough qualifying before the buyers ever look at the first house, as it is the only way the buying prospects and the salesperson can intelligently decide what properties should be shown. Further explain how you will research the marketplace and research the different financing options available. If possible, begin the qualification process at the open house, and set a firm appointment time for them to meet you at your office or the office of a competent loan officer to get the process started.

Prospecting Future File Candidates

Future File Candidates: Property owners planning to sell but not ready to place their property on the market at this time. The following reaction is typical of those you will encounter when "Prospecting Future File Candidates."

Ring, ring, ring. "Mr. Johnson, this is Jim Londay with Jim Londay and Associates. You were referred to me by your brother Bill. He indicated you are considering selling your house in the spring." Mr. Johnson: "Uh, yes, I am, but I am really not even sure if we are going to sell or not, and if we do, we are not even sure it will be in the spring." Salesperson: "Mr. Johnson, with your permission, I would like to arrange two visits with you. The first is to look at your property and the second to present a market analysis to tell you the approximate current value of your property and what you would net from a sale at that price." Mr. Johnson: "I do not believe I am ready for that. We do not even know if we are going to sell or not." In this situation, use the approach described in the previous section on FSBOs.

Open-Ended Questions for Sellers

The following are a list of questions you can ask prospective sellers, whether they be FSBOs, owners of expired listings, duty calls or any other selling prospects you may find. These will help you maintain control and allow you quickly to learn more about your sellers' needs and concerns.

For Owners of For-Sale-By-Owner Properties

1. What are you asking for your house?
2. What terms are you offering to prospective buyers?
3. What kind of response have you received from your advertising?
4. Do you know how to qualify buyers?
5. Do you have a full understanding of how discount points work?
6. Have you arranged for an attorney to handle your sale?

For Owners of Expired Listings

1. Why do you feel the house did not sell?
2. What do you feel your property is worth?
3. How did you arrive at that figure?

For Sellers in General

1. What have you liked most about living in this house? If I know what is most important to you, I can perhaps use that to convince buyers this is the correct house for them.
2. What have your utility bills been?
3. Have you made any improvements to the house I cannot see that could add to its value, such as added insulation?
4. Are there any problems with the house that are not readily apparent when a person walks through and looks at it?
5. What one aspect of your house do you feel makes it most desirable to a buyer?
6. In your opinion, what is the biggest objection a potential buyer would have to buying this particular property? This can be quite effective in getting your sellers to acknowledge they do have a specific location, condition or terms problem.
7. What are your plans once you sell?
8. When would be the optimum time for you to give possession of this property?

6

Closing When Listing

The following are specific objections you may encounter when attempting to list a property.

"I want to list this house for only 60 days."

Listing a property for an unreasonably short period of time does not provide enough time to correctly market the property, thus shortchanging the sellers. In addition, it does not give you and your broker a fair chance to get a return on your investment of time and money. The minimum time you should list a property should be one and a half times the average marketing time for the area. For example, if the average time on the market is 80 days, you should get a minimum of a 120-day listing. The reason for this is that there is time and money involved, both yours and your broker's, in listing a property.

Misguided sellers often have the impression that if they list their property for a short period of time, the listing salesperson and broker will work harder to produce a quick sale. Several articles in consumer magazines suggest as much. The following approach, used with the permission of your sales manager, is very effective:

"Mrs. Cornielson, I understand your desire to have a short listing period. You do not want to tie yourself into a long-term obligation with a broker with whom you may not be satisfied. I would like to make this proposal: Let's agree to have the same working relationship I have with all of my sellers. I want you to work with me because you feel I am doing a good job for you. For that reason, I will terminate this listing at no cost, no questions asked, the day you are unhappy with the services I am providing. If you like, I will add this in writing to our listing agreement. In effect, you are not really signing a 120-day listing. You are signing what is, essentially, a one-day listing because that will be all the time it will take for me to terminate the listing."

If you are doing a good job, it is unlikely the sellers will terminate this listing. As long as you are providing a service that these sellers want, need and deserve, they are not going to be asking to terminate these listings.

Your protection against the small percentage of dishonest people is the "If sold to someone due to the broker's efforts clause" most brokers have in their listing agreements. These clauses normally state that if the seller sells the house within so many days after termination of the listing (I suggest a minimum of 180 days) to a buyer generated during the listing period, the seller still owes a commission. It is in a broker's best interest to have this clause in the listings. The following is an easy way to explain this clause and remove its sting.

"Mrs. Cornielson, there is a clause in this listing agreement that you possibly could find offensive. I would like to explain it to you. It is called a protection clause, and it says that if you sell your house to any buyer found during the listing period, you still owe a listing commission. Now I know and you know that you would never purposely cheat me. However, it is our company policy to have this as part of every agreement, and if it is not in there, I have to answer to my sales manager. The only reason it is in there is because it is our policy and not because I distrust you in any way."

"We want to find the house we want to buy before we list ours." "Mr. and Mrs. Francis, it is natural for a couple selling one home and buying another to think they will sell their house before finding the right house for themselves, leaving them high and dry. This is an understandable fear. However, these sellers are putting themselves in a situation that is almost certain to cost them thousands of dollars if they insist on finding the house they want to buy before listing theirs. Let me explain the different ways this can work. You find your dream house. You are ready to buy it and want to write up an offer contingent upon your house selling within 60 days. Most sellers will not seriously consider this type of offer. If they do accept the offer, you have in most every case exhausted almost, if not all, of your negotiating chips. The sellers may say, 'I am running a big risk taking my house off the market for 60 days when I am not even sure they are going to get theirs sold. I am certainly not going to negotiate price, terms, condition or anything else.' If you find a seller who will accept a contract contingent upon your house selling, you will usually end up paying more for the house than otherwise. Buyers may say, 'If the sellers of my dream house are going to react like that, I just won't buy their house.' Thinking the sellers of the dream house are going to disregard their poor negotiating position is unrealistic. You are not in control of the sellers' actions. The motivations of the other parties involved must be considered if you are to structure the best end result.

"Another problem may be encountered if the contingency offer is accepted. In addition to frequently paying more for the house, you are forcing yourself to produce a quick sale of your current home that may net you less than you should get. You will have at most 60 days to find a buyer for your house, as you naturally want to avoid double payments or interim financing. Owners in this situation are forced to price their house aggressively if they are to have any chance of selling and closing in 60 days. They feel obligated to take the first offer that comes by and lose on both ends.

"A second approach is to find your dream house and buy it even though yours is not listed and then obtain interim financing for the period of time it takes to sell and close your house. This also has its flaws. Houses are currently taking 12 weeks to sell in the metropolitan area. It takes about another six weeks to close. We are looking at an average of 18 weeks between the time your house is listed and the time you get your proceeds. That is four and a half months. If you buy and close on your dream house and obtain interim financing before listing yours, you are most likely setting yourself up for four or more months of double payments. In the price range you are considering, that is more than $4,000. I cannot in good conscience advise that you buy and sell a house using this approach.

"I have known a number of people who have used interim financing and said, 'We can afford the double payments. It is not going to be a problem.' They are optimistic their house will sell quickly. After two months of making double payments, however, they feel an incredible amount of pressure. They then bail out of their old house at less than they could have received because they are negotiating from a weak position.

"A critical factor in obtaining the most for your house is having enough marketing time to find that one 'right buyer' willing to pay top dollar. To resolve your concerns, I suggest the following: Let's put your house on the market immediately and aggressively promote it. At the same time, we will start looking at properties in the price range and areas that interest you. In this way, if we find a buyer for your house before you find the perfect dream house, you will be prepared to go out and make a decision on very short notice. I have never had a situation where the sellers sold their house and were unable to find their dream house.

"If this is still a concern of yours and if someone wants to buy your house before you find your 'perfect' house, we can insert a clause saying the sale of your house is contingent upon your finding a suitable house to buy within five days or a week.

"In the event that you do find your dream house before a buyer is found for yours, you can then consider obtaining interim financing with the knowledge that your house is already on the market. The initial period of time it takes to get it into the multiple-listing service and into the advertising system has already passed, and you have saved yourself one to three months of double expenses by already having the sale of your house in the works. Your feelings and anxiety are natural and understandable. However, the risk-gain factor is such that you really have more to risk in insisting you find the right house before you list yours than you have to gain."

Answering Objections to FHA/VA Financing

Seller does not want to offer FHA and VA terms for fear of making repairs. You can use the following approach when the sellers understand the necessity to pay discount points but fear selling the house FHA and VA because of anticipated repairs.

"Mr. and Mrs. Wilson, I understand your fear of potential repairs. You do have an older house, and an FHA or VA appraiser may request repairs. In my opinion, if repairs are required, they will be minor in nature. If they are not, there is built-in protection for the sellers on every FHA and VA sale. We commonly refer to it as the *VA* or *FHA Escape Clause*, wherein the buyers and/or sellers can withdraw from the agreement with no penalty if the property does not appraise for the agreed-upon price. If the appraisal comes back at less than full price, you can rescind the original agreement. Required repairs also allow you to back out of the contract. If you feel the repairs are excessive, you are under no obligation to complete the transaction. Of course, if you decide to take this option, we will need to return the buyers' earnest money and place the property back on the market in an effort to find another buyer.

"By allowing us to offer FHA and VA terms, we are opening your house to a larger number of buyers, buyers who could not otherwise purchase your property. This is done at no extra liability to you because of the safety afforded under the *VA* and *FHA Escape Clauses.*"

Try this approach if the house in such a poor condition that the FHA and VA are certain to require repairs.

"Tom and Jill, there is a strong likelihood that an FHA or VA appraiser will require you to make repairs on your property. Naturally, you don't want to do this, but the alternatives are surely worse. If you do not offer FHA and VA terms, you are eliminating many excellent buyers for your property. In fact, the most likely buyers for this house will only be able to buy a house if they buy FHA or VA. We want to offer this property to the greatest number of potential buyers who can net you what you need. You have indicated that you want the highest net possible. To do this, you will have to make these repairs and improvements. It is best to make these improvements, allowing us to offer good terms and sell the property at top dollar."

"*I don't want to offer FHA and VA terms because I don't want to pay discount points. I do not see why I should subsidize the buyers' loan. If they want to go FHA or VA, let them pay for the discount points themselves.*"

"Joe and Mary Fran, I understand how you feel. Discount points at today's quotes for this property run about $2,400, and no one wants to subtract that amount from the proceeds of their property. But I would first like you to read this explanation of how discount points work, and then I have some additional information I would like you to consider." (Give them a copy of "How Discount Points Work." See example 5.A.)

"Now that you have a basic understanding of how discount points work, I would like you to look at your house from the buyers' viewpoint. From the buyers' viewpoint, FHA and VA loans offer a list of advantages that are hard to pass up. There is no or very little down payment. Most homebuyers in this range do not have the 20 percent down payment required to obtain a conventional loan. If they cannot buy FHA or VA, they cannot even consider buying a house.

"Other advantages include an interest rate on FHA and VA loans that are less than the going conventional interest rates. There is no prepayment penalty, and these loans are easily assumed with only minor restrictions and costs." (Note: a release of liability is required on FHA loans placed after December 1, 1986, if they are assumed within two years of when the loan was made. Further restrictions apply, and you should check with an approved FHA lender.) "For all of these reasons, FHA and VA loans are not only highly popular with but sometimes an absolute requirement for many buyers. I recently completed a market study that showed more than 68 percent of the houses sold in the price range of your house were financed with new FHA or VA financing. You are cutting out two-thirds of the buyers in the marketplace if you do not offer FHA and VA terms. If you cut out two-thirds of the buyers in your marketplace, it will in all likelihood take three times as long to sell your property. The studies referred to on the sheet I gave you indicate that most, if not all, of the costs of points are brought back to the sellers in the form of a higher sales price. These reasons add up to one conclusion: It is in the sellers' best interest to offer FHA and VA terms if their house is in this price range and area of town."

Sellers do not want to make repairs required by VA or FHA in order to close a pending sale. This is relatively easy to overcome. All you have to do is explain the options to the sellers. They are simple. Either complete the repairs and close the sale, or place the property back on the market. Placing the property back on the market presents the sellers with multiple problems. First of all, no one knows when the next buyers will come. Second, even if we do find other buyers, if they request the same type of financing, we are stuck with the original appraisal for six months if it was an FHA or VA sale. Third, if buyers are found requesting a different type of loan, the chances are good the same problems will arise again. Fourth, there is a compensating factor of the extra money it is going to cost the sellers in the form of principle, interest, taxes, insurance, maintenance and repairs until the next buyers are found.

This is a form of "alternative choice" where your sellers have two bad choice selections. They can do the repairs and have a minor financial loss or back out of the sale, put the property back on the market and take the chance of losing more money.

Objections Regarding Commission Rates

"Seven percent is an awful lot of money. Will you negotiate your commission?"

"Tom and Cindy, I understand how you feel. Seven percent amounts to real money. I work for a full-service broker. You have seen my marketing plan and you agree it is quite aggressive and more complete than anything anyone else has shown you. All of these promotional programs cost money, money that brokers can't spend if they reduce their fees. If I reduce our fee and delete these marketing programs, I will not be able to do what I feel is an adequate job of marketing your property.

"Another factor I would like you to consider is that a broker's fee is divided in a number of ways. It is divided among the listing broker, the listing salesperson, the selling broker and the selling salesperson. In addition, there are closing fees, advertising money and processing fees that come out of this commission. What each party in the transaction gets is actually far less than seven percent.

"The company I work for has a simple policy. If I take a listing at less than seven percent, any reduction I give the sellers comes out of my part of the commission. Since I only get a fraction of this commission, if I went down to six percent, I would not be making enough to make selling your property worthwhile. The price of someone's services is important, but the price must be considered in the context of the extent and quality of services the customer receives. If you want the quickest sale with the highest net, it is in your best interest to list your property with a broker who offers a broad, aggressive marketing program. However, if the price you pay is your only consideration, you will want to list your house with someone other than me, as there are brokers who will take your listing at a discount. Real estate brokers are like any other business people. They charge the price their services will bring in the marketplace. The best full-service brokers in this area charge and get seven percent. Those who will reduce their commission are, in effect, saying they are not good enough to list properties at the same rate charged by the best brokers in the city.

"Yes, it is true you can list your property with other brokers at six percent or five percent or even less with some discount brokers, but the services you will receive will be correspondingly fewer. My job is to find a buyer who will pay top dollar for this house. To do that, I will spend serious amounts of time and money. For these reasons, I cannot reduce my commission."

I used the following alternate approach with a hard-bargaining insurance executive with great success. This selling prospect liked my marketing program, liked the company I worked for and didn't even quibble about what I thought his house was worth. This was an individual who "never paid retail for anything in his life" and was determined to get me to make a special concession for him in the form of a reduced commission rate. In a pleasant and civilized way, he tried for more than half an hour to convince me to reduce my commission. Of course, this was not going to happen, as I will walk away from a listing rather than cut my pay. I eventually tried the following approach out of desperation:

"Steve, you work for an insurance company, and I am sure you have a superior to whom you must answer. Imagine your boss coming to you tomorrow and saying, 'Jim Londay is thinking about buying a group policy for all of his employees at his small manufacturing company. He likes the coverage. He thinks the agent is going to give him good service. He likes the stability and size of our company and feels we can pay any claims he may have. He has just one concern. The first year's premium is $7,000 and he only wants to pay $6,300. Steve, is it all right with you if we take this $700 out of your paycheck this month?'

"Steve, that is what you are asking me to do, and I am not going to do it, even if it means not listing your house." I put the agreement down on the table, placed the pen on it and did not say a word. He picked it up and signed.

One last approach is to explain how your marketing program and your negotiating skills will in all probability bring more in the form of net dollars to your sellers than they would be able to receive by listing their property with someone else.

SPECIFIC OBJECTIONS AND SOLUTIONS WHEN LISTING

"We only want you to show the house three nights a week and Sunday afternoons."

"Bill and Mary Kay, one of the basics of selling success is to sell when the buyer is ready to buy, not when it is convenient for the seller to sell. If we set strict limits on when the property can be shown, we are going to eliminate many excellent prospects. By limiting when we can show the house, you are stifling us in our efforts to get the property sold in a timely fashion. I would like you to reconsider this and give us free access to the house throughout the week, unless there is a specific emergency or problem in showing the house at a specific time."

"We like your program but your company, Archie Realty, is relatively small. Jim Londay and Associates is very strong in this area. Why should we list with you rather than him, when there are so many more of his signs around town than yours?"

"Jim's agents do a very good job. However, I do not feel you should pick the listing salesperson by the name of the company. The salesperson who lists and promotes your house is a bigger determining factor on how quickly it sells than the company's name. Yes, the company I work for is not as large as some other companies, but I believe the service I give and the promotional program I have outlined for you will far exceed what you will get from any other salesperson or agency. If you focus on what I am going to do to market your house, you will find it hard to find someone who can beat my program."

"I am ready to list my house with you. However, I have a potential buyer, and I would hate to list my house with you until I know whether this person is serious or not."

"That is a valid point, but we have a solution for that, Michelle and Tim. I can list your property at this time and still protect you by including a two-week exclusion for your potential buyers in the listing agreement. We will put a clause in the listing stating that if you sell your house to this specific couple anytime in the next two weeks, you can sell it direct to them and not pay a commission. This will protect you in case your specific buyers decide to purchase your house and will also allow us to immediately begin our marketing efforts on your property. We will not lose valuable time waiting on the chance that these buyers may purchase the property."

"I am ready to list, but I have a for-sale-by-owner open-house ad in the paper for this coming Sunday. I will have to wait until Monday to list the property with you."

"If that is your only objection, may I suggest the following: 'Let's list the property now. I will hold your scheduled open house and will reimburse you for the cost of your ad. In addition, I will promote the open house through other channels. This will allow us to start the entire marketing process and get it into the multiple-listing book before this week's deadline is past and still make sure the money you spent on that ad is not wasted."

"You are not the first salesperson to say you have a buyer. I am not going to list it with you for no good reason."

"Daniel and Susan, some salespeople may have told you they had a buying prospect for your house when they did not. I have what I think is a legitimate buyer for your house. I would like to propose what we call a one-party listing. You list it with me with the listing contract being valid only for the one specifically named buyer I have. If I do have a buyer, your house will be sold. If my buyer does not like your house, you are still able to sell your property on your own without paying a commission."

LISTING FOR SALE BY OWNERS

For Sale By Owners have two objections that must be addressed before you can list their property. The first is "You cannot do anything for me that I cannot do for myself." The second is "I am going to save the commission." There is a grain of truth to both of these statements, but just a grain. The sellers contend they can have a lawyer write up the contract and a title insurance company close the sale for a mere two or three hundred dollars. They claim they can order a survey and a termite inspection just as easily as the broker. They assume that is what we do to earn our commission. They are wrong. We get paid for producing a buyer who is willing to pay top market value. Filling out the forms and arranging the closing is just paperwork.

This objection can be handled by explaining to the seller what we do for the buyer. Carefully outline the entire process a salesperson goes through when working with a buyer. Explain the qualifying process, researching the marketplace, arranging the showings, showing the property, writing up the sale, negotiating the agreement, getting the loan approved and arranging and handling the closing. Also explain how the salesperson will protect the buyer's rights with full disclosure, even though all the licensees, in most instances, represent the seller. The buyer ultimately pays for these services in the form of a higher sales price, as property sold through real estate agents normally brings a higher price than those sold FSBO.

Continue with dialogue similar to the following. "Sellers receive more when working through a broker because the most desirable buyers ordinarily work with real estate salespeople. Out-of-town buyers are the best buyers available as they are highly motivated, usually have money to work with and almost always work with an agent. Out-of-towners almost never look at FSBOs. Since first-time buyers frequently lack the self-confidence, experience and knowledge to buy a property directly from an owner, they usually work with real estate salespeople also. Buyers who decide to move when they outgrow their starter homes also tend to work with salespeople. Twenty years down the road, empty-nesters who are eager to sell that 3,000-square-foot two-story and move into a smaller home or a condo almost always work with salespeople.

"But we do not have all of the buyers, Daniel and Susan. There are groups of buyers who look at FSBOs. The largest group consists of investors. Investors look at FSBOs because they do not want to pay what the property is worth. Another group of people seeking out FSBOs includes devotees of 'buy real estate with no-money-down seminars.' They are looking for a steal. Unqualified buyers also look at FSBOs. When prospective buyers are so poorly qualified that a real estate salesperson will not work with them, they will commonly try to 'prove that salesperson wrong' and try to buy a FSBO. After all, everybody that they have ever asked has given them credit before. Even though they have seven credit cards with maximum balances, they do not see why a lender is not going to give them a house loan. Daniel and Susan, investors, people who buy real estate with no money down and unqualified buyers are the people who look at FSBOs, and I do not think you want to sell to any of those people."

The following three quotes are quite effective when talking to FSBOs.

"Daniel and Susan, the plain fact is, agents control and work with the majority of the qualified buyers."

"The only buyers who look at FSBO properties are bargain hunters and people so unqualified, no agent will work with them."

"Most sellers find they need to list with an agent if they are to find a buyer at or near the top of the fair range."

I'm Going to Save the Commission

Countering the objection, "We are going to save the commission," is quite easy. Explain the costs they will incur if they do succeed in selling the house themselves. Start by taking a blank sheet of paper and writing what the commission on their house would be. Label it "Potential Savings."

"Daniel and Susan, the reason you want to sell your property yourselves is to save the commission. I understand that. Seven percent is a lot of money. If you could actually sell your house and save seven percent, I would be all for you, but in most cases that simply does not happen. This figure is your potential savings. When a FSBO is lucky enough to generate an offer, the buyer normally says, 'Let's split the savings.' Deduct half of the commission savings on your worksheet.

"You also have to pay for your own advertising. Average time on the market for listed houses is 12 weeks. Successful sales by owners rarely do as well, but let's say you sell your property in 12 weeks. You are spending approximately $60 a week on advertising. That means if you do sell it in 12 weeks, there is another $720 out of your proceeds.

"Let's say you find a buyer. You are going to have to pay an attorney or title company to write up the sale and handle the closing. This can be another $300. (Use a figure appropriate to your locale.) On top of this, most buyers of FSBO properties are investors and they will insist on an additional concession on the price before they will buy. Most often, this last final concession will wipe out the last of your potential savings.

"*Daniel and Susan, many FSBOs end up losing more in the form of advertising, negotiating and closing the sale than the very commission they started out to save.*"

After explaining the above two objections, go through a list of all of the advantages of working with an agent. That includes having access to the most desirable buyers and getting their house in the multiple-listing service. Sellers also benefit from our financing knowledge and sources and can frequently save money when asked to assist with the buyers' financing. All showings are expertly conducted and the listing broker acts as a negotiating buffer. There is also an element of safety included, as our buyers are prequalified and accompanied to your home by an agent. Also, there are never any missed prospects when a property is listed, as buying prospects can always find an agent to give them information on the listed property. Sellers of all listed properties benefit from agency advertising. If the perfect buyers for their property answer any ad in the paper, the system will match your property with the correct buyers. There is also the additional savings in advertising and closing fees, as well as a saving in time, as the broker takes care of all of the hassles (see *List for Success* for more in-depth techniques when working with FSBOs).

7

Earning the Sellers' Cooperation

The foundation of a quick sale is in place at the time of the listing. The following are the four basic steps that must be completed to list the property correctly. This is the first half of the "Seller Education Process." The second part, covered later in the chapter, is obtaining feedback from salespeople and buying prospects during the marketing period, and educating the sellers on how to best change their marketing plan to get the property sold.

Educating the Seller During the Listing Presentation

Introduction to basic marketing principles. This is the first phase in my four-step plan (see chapter 2). I suggest copying the marketing principles summarized on pages 26–28 in chapter 2, and giving them to your sellers at the measure-up appointment. Ask the property owners to review the basic principles before you come back to present your market analysis. Review of these marketing principles will be the first phase of the market analysis you complete. This is necessary, as your sellers will find it difficult to make intelligent decisions on how to market their house without a basic understanding of how the marketplace works.

Start your explanation like this: "Frank and Priscilla, there are a number of basic marketing principles that apply to all residential sales. Before we start discussing your house specifically, I would like to share these marketing principles with you, so you can better make a decision as to how to market your house."

Proceed to explain the basic marketing principles, stressing the principles that most apply to your sellers. If your sellers have condition problems, spend enough time on condition so they will see their house as buyers would. Spend whatever time is necessary to make sure they fully understand what you are talking about.

Proceed and spend as much time as applicable on each section of the marketing principles. This will give your sellers a good basis for understanding your recommendations.

Market data.   The second phase of the seller-education process during the listing presentation is a thorough explanation of the market data that has a direct bearing on your sellers' property. This includes solds, pending sales, expireds and current on the markets. If your multiple—listing service is computerized, a computer summary of market activity, including average time on the market, average amount or percentage of negotiation, percentage of listings expired and percentage of houses listed that sell in any one week should be explained.

The prospective sellers' house should be compared individually with each single sold, pending, expired and relevant on the market. Only by taking the time to do this will your sellers begin to see where their property fits in the marketplace.

Reaching agreement on offering price, terms and condition. Successful completion of this third phase is crucial. This is where you must convince the sellers to put the property on the market in a marketable condition, offering competitive terms, at a price that will attract a buyer. This is one of the biggest challenges in listing or selling real estate. How well you do here will be a reflection of your level of effectiveness and expertise. For further information on this phase, we suggest you read chapter 7 of *List for Success.*

During this phase of the listing presentation, ask your sellers to call you anytime they have a concern or question, no matter how slight. This is done for two reasons: First, we want to keep concerns minor and not let them grow into a major headache for the sellers. Second, every time we get our sellers to call us about a concern or question on marketing a property, it gives us yet another opportunity to continue the seller-education process.

The five-week marketing schedule. The fourth phase is outlining your marketing plan for the first five weeks of the listing period. Without question, it is in the property owners' best interests to sell the property in the first four to six weeks. The longer the property is on the market, the less your sellers will net through added expenses and lower price in most instances. I use a five-week marketing plan because that amount of time will allow you to put your promotional programs into place and test the waters. You will obtain enough marketplace feedback within five weeks to allow you to determine if a change in marketing approach is needed.

After completion of your explanation of the marketing schedule, try dialogue something like the following: "Sandy and Ryan, the reason I have outlined a marketing plan for only five weeks is simple. The response we get in the first five weeks will tell us how to market the property in the second five weeks if the property is still unsold. Experience has shown us that if a property is not sold in the first five weeks on the market, it means the sellers will usually have to make a significant adjustment in either price, terms or condition to produce a buyer. That is why I have outlined such an aggressive marketing program for the first five weeks you will be on the market. As we discussed earlier, properties that sell the fastest usually sell for the most money. It is my sincere hope that we will get the property sold in the first five weeks. If not, it will be time for us to get together and discuss what progress we have had to date and what we are going to do to market the property for the next five weeks. If market response has been favorable, I may suggest no changes, just a continuation of the current marketing efforts. However, if there has been a clear signal from the marketplace that we need to make an adjustment in either price, terms or condition, I will show you the data I have collected, give you my best advice and let you decide how we should proceed."

The seller-education process during the marketing period.   This is done by obtaining all marketplace feedback and getting it to your sellers in a written form as quickly as possible. By doing this, your sellers will learn how salespeople and prospective buyers view the sellers' property. We are using the marketplace feedback to get our sellers to see their property from the buyers' perspective.

All feedback should be put in writing to obtain the maximum positive benefit. The human mind has an incredible capacity to dismiss and forget anything it does not want to hear or believe. It is very easy for the sellers to forget negative feedback we have provided them about their property. Sellers are likely to block out verbal negative feedback such as: the buyers think their house is overpriced or that there was a pet odor in the family room or that their offering terms are unacceptable. This is a defense mechanism used by all sellers from time to time. By compiling and keeping marketplace feedback, we are collecting written proof of the reasons why their property is not selling. Let's see how this is done.

Tour feedback.   Going on tour makes salespeople more effective when both listing and selling properties. To sell houses, you need to know what is available. You cannot obtain enough information about real estate from a multiple-listing book to describe the property to a person calling for information from a sign or an ad. On occasion, I have had buyers for whom I could not find a house no matter how long I pored through the book. I would go on tour and amazingly see that the house that was just right for my buyer was there.

Tours are particularly valuable for new salespeople. I suggest new salespeople go on tour with an experienced salesperson. People who have been in this business for two years or longer have a wealth of information that can be tapped by a new salesperson. Go on tour with an old pro and ask questions.

In addition to keeping you up-to-date on what is available on the market, the tour can provide valuable feedback for your sellers. There are two things a listing salesperson can do on a tour to educate one's sellers. The first is to obtain a tour price average. If your company is small and all salespeople tour every listing, I suggest that they record on a blank sheet what they feel is the true market value of each house. An average is then compiled by a staff member and forwarded to your sellers. If you work for a larger company where not all salespeople look at every listing on tour, the listing salesperson should pick up the cards of the salespeople who did tour the house, call them up and come up with a tour average. Whichever approach is used, give the tour average in writing to your sellers, with an explanation that the tour average is often remarkably close to the eventual sales price of a property.

Second, you can solicit constructive comments from salespeople who toured the property. This can be particularly valuable when your sellers refuse to acknowledge or correct specific problems. Summarize the salespeople's comments on paper. For example: "Agent A liked the decorating and the landscaping in the back yard, but felt there was too much furniture in the family room, giving it a cluttered look. Agent B suggested painting the living room, dining room and hall, and cleaning the family-room carpet, as a pet odor was detected." Collect feedback from four, five or six salespeople. Type them neatly and get them to your sellers. In most cases, your sellers are understanding. It is not you who is telling them their house is in poor condition or that it is overpriced. You are merely the messenger, bringing them news from other experts in the field. Tour feedback can nurture the seeds of marketplace knowledge you planted at the listing presentation.

Open-house feedback.   This usually provides the first feedback from prospective buyers the sellers receive. To most effectively do this, bring a tablet with a sheet of carbon paper to the house. As the open-house visitors leave, summarize their positive and negative comments and their views on the market value of the property. It would go something like this. Couple A: "Valid buying prospects. Their lease is up in six weeks, and they are seriously considering buying a house. Positive comments: Liked the neighborhood and the basic floor plan of the house. Negative comments: Felt there was a considerable amount of cosmetic work needed. Their comments lead me to believe they think the entire interior needs to be repainted and the carpeting needs to be replaced. I asked them what they felt the market value of your property was, and they said they would not pay more than $84,000 or $85,000 for it."

Summarize the comments of every individual or group that views the property. Leave the original on the kitchen table. Put the carbon in your file.

Thanks for showing my listing.   This is a brief questionnaire that is to be mailed to every salesperson who shows one of your listings. Enclose a self-addressed, stamped envelope so the showing salesperson merely has to fill in the comments and drop it back in the mail. I get about a two-thirds response rate. Upon receiving a completed "Thanks for showing my listing" (see example 7.A), make a copy for your file and drop the original in the mail.

The most powerful question is "Why did your prospects not buy this house?" Your sellers may be upset, angry or even outraged at some of the comments, but it is imperative for your sellers to acknowledge the problems their property faces when competing with similar properties on the market.

Chapter Summary

Help your sellers obtain the HQF by repeatedly educating them to basic marketing principles and providing them with continual feedback from salespeople who have shown their house and from prospective buyers who have looked at it.

EXAMPLE 7.A
"THANKS FOR SHOWING MY LISTING!"

(Place a copy of the photo and data sheet
from the MLS book here.)

Thanks for showing the above property located at: _____

The owner and I would appreciate your frank feedback. Please provide us with the following to the extent of your knowledge.

What did your prospect think the house was worth? _____

What do you feel the market value is? _____

If known, please state why your prospect didn't buy this house: ____

_____

_____

_____

Do you have any suggestions to improve the marketability of the property?

_____

_____

_____

The source of this information will be kept strictly confidential. Please return your comments in the enclosed stamped envelope. Your assistance in helping us market this property correctly is appreciated.

Sincerely,

8

Obtaining Adjustments While on the Market

There are many times during the marketing period when it becomes apparent a property will not sell at the original listed price, terms and condition. Once the marketplace has told you "we're not interested!" whatever form it takes, it is time for action. A major part of our job is to truthfully inform our sellers how they stand in the marketplace. We need to get our sellers to see the necessity of adjustments once it becomes obvious the property is unsaleable as currently marketed. The following occasions are the most likely times that call for an adjustment in price, terms or condition.

At the listing: Your market analysis indicates the top of the fair range for a property is $110,000. You want to list it at $110,000. Your sellers insist on $115,000. A prearranged price adjustment is the best solution to this problem. If possible, get the sellers to market the property at $115,000 with a clause in the listing stating the price will be adjusted to $110,000 if the property is not sold by an agreed-upon time period, preferably within four weeks.

After the tour: If tour feedback is uniformly negative regarding price, terms or condition, an adjustment must be made. Do not wait for the end of the initial five-week marketing period to meet with your sellers to respond to this sure sign that a change is in order.

After an open house: If open-house traffic was disappointing, or again, if negative feedback was received from the prospective buyers going through the property, then an adjustment should be recommended.

After five weeks: You explained to the sellers at the time you listed their property that you would meet with them after five weeks to discuss how the property should be marketed in the next five weeks. They are expecting you to come back, and the stage is set for an adjustment. Get an adjustment here or risk losing control.

No showings: No showings in the first five weeks indicate one thing: The price is too high. Absolutely no activity means every salesperson and every buyer who looked in the multiple-listing service shared the same opinion: This property is not even worth looking at. The only remedy for no showings is a significant adjustment in price.

Lots of showings, no offers: This usually indicates a condition or a location problem not apparent from looking at the multiple-listing service book. Something is turning the buyers off. Feedback from the tour, the open house and all showings should be evaluated to find the specific reason buyers are looking at the property and crossing it off their lists.

Lost good buyer to another house: An excellent time to obtain an adjustment is after your sellers have lost a good prospect to another house on the marketplace.

After low offers: A series of low offers is a strong indication the asking price is too high. Although done subconsciously, many buyers underbid what they feel the market value is by the amount they feel the property is overpriced. If the property is worth $130,000 and it is listed at $140,000, it is likely most offers will come in around $120,000. A good time to obtain adjustments is immediately after receiving a substantially low offer.

Seller deadline approaching: Sellers may feel they have all the time in the world when the moving date is four months away. Under these circumstances, your sellers frequently lack real motivation. As their planned moving date approaches, they will become more serious about doing what it takes to sell their property.

When the sellers call and are upset because of a lack of market activity: If your sellers call and they are upset, they are subconsciously asking for two things. One is "Help. I need your help. I have to sell this house." The second thing they are saying in an indirect way is "We are ready to take whatever steps are necessary to sell this property at this time." There is no better time to obtain adjustments.

Gathering Data for the Adjustment Appointment

To increase your chances of getting the type and size of adjustment you want, you need to build and prepare a convincing case for the adjustment. To strengthen your case, compile the following material:

1. The five-week results review (see example 8.A).
2. Updated market data: solds, pendings, expireds and on the markets. Also update market statistics, such as number of expireds and average time sold.
3. All marketplace feedback discussed in chapter 6, tour feedback, open-house feedback and showing feedback.
4. A list of things you want to adjust, whether it be price, terms or condition.
5. New sellers' estimate sheets if you are asking for a price adjustment.
6. Forms for making an adjustment in your listing.

EXAMPLE 8.A

THE FIVE-WEEK RESULTS REVIEW

This self-test was designed for the use of real estate listing agents and/or owners of properties for sale. Its purpose is to help the agent or owners more clearly focus on how the marketplace is responding to the combined marketing efforts of the owners and their agent. This serves as a guide as to whether an adjustment in price, terms or condition is called for.

	Yes	No
Has a written offer been received on the property in the last five weeks?	___	___
Has there been an adjustment of five percent or more in the listing price in the last five weeks?	___	___
Has the condition of the property been significantly improved in the last five weeks?	___	___
Have offering terms that are more attractive to potential buyers been added in the last five weeks?	___	___
Is there a qualified buying prospect interested in the property at the present time?	___	___

Four or five "No" answers strongly indicate that a change in marketing strategy will be necessary to produce a sale. The basic options of every seller are to adjust the price, add more favorable terms or improve the condition of the property. Keep in mind that location, condition and offering terms are all a function of price. Market studies have shown that if market activity is unproductive for a period of five weeks, it is unlikely that a sale will occur in the next five weeks unless an adjustment in price, terms or condition is made.

The Adjustment Appointment

"The Adjustment Appointment" begins by jointly filling out the five-week results review. Explain all data in detail, i.e., compare your sellers' house with every final sold, every pending, every expired and every on the market. Also compare your sellers' house with average time on the market, average percent of sale negotiated from listing price to sales price and the ratio of on the markets and solds in the last week.

Continue by reviewing all compiled marketplace feedback. Your sellers are often distressed when reviewing the material, but it is important for them to see their house the way buyers and salespeople view it in order for them to successfully market it. Once you have reviewed all of this data, it is time for you to get out your written list of suggestions for adjustments. I would like to share some general thoughts on obtaining adjustments. The first is that we need to place the burden of this decision where it belongs: on the sellers. Although sellers consider our advice, they ultimately make the final decision. Use dialogue somewhat like the following:

"Bill and Rose, as the sellers you will now decide how quickly your property is going to sell by the type and size of the adjustments you make. My broker and I are doing everything reasonably possible to promote this property. We have been on the market long enough and have received enough feedback for us to know it will not sell at the current price, terms and condition. We will, of course, continue our marketing efforts, but it is likely they will be fruitless unless we adjust to the marketplace and get closer to what buyers are looking for. *The more significant adjustments you make, the faster your property sells. The less significant adjustments you make, the slower it sells. If the adjustments are not significant, your property will remain unsaleable.*"

Specific Objections and Solutions
When Obtaining Adjustments

"We only want to reduce the price $1,000." "I understand how you feel, Rose and Bill, but if we were only $1,000 off, the property would sell. If we were that close, we would be generating acceptable offers. Generally speaking, the marketplace does not recognize any adjustments of less than five percent." Your sellers will look up toward the ceiling, and you can see them mentally calculating/$80,000 at five percent, and then blurt, out, "You want us to reduce it $4,000!?" You calmly reply, "Actually, I was thinking more like $5,000." Ask for a major adjustment, and

leave enough room to compromise and still get a large enough adjustment to get the job done.

"*Instead of painting and replacing the carpets, let's give the buyers an allowance and let them pick out their own colors and carpeting.*"

"Rose and Bill, in theory this works fine. However, as I explained when I first listed your house, people buy houses based on emotion and not logic. It is easy for a buyer to walk into a house, see and smell the new carpeting, observe freshly painted walls and fall in love with the property. It is easy to get passionate about a recently redecorated house. It is more difficult for a buyer to get emotionally involved with a property that needs work, and a few words in small type in the multiple-listing book that say '$800 carpeting and paint allowance.' Let's spend the money in a way that will create a real impact and do what we can to turn the buyers on."

"*I have to have $24,000 out of this house to move to Florida and close on the house I am buying in Ft. Lauderdale.*"

We are often faced with sellers who "have to have" a certain amount of money. If we have been in the marketplace long enough to know we cannot get $24,000, we have an ethical and moral obligation to tell our sellers we cannot do it. Try something like this.

"Brad and Stephanie, I know your situation, and I know you feel you need $24,000 out of the sale of this house to complete your move and purchase of your new house. Unfortunately, what you need out of this house has no relationship with its market value and what we can net out of it.

"We have been on the market long enough and obtained enough feedback for me to tell you with certainty that we cannot obtain the $24,000 you need. That leaves you with two choices: One, you can find a way to sell this house and complete your move with approximately $20,000, which, in my opinion, is the most we can get, or two, you can decide not to sell your house and stay here. That's not what you want to hear, but I feel an obligation to put the cards on the table and let you know what your options are, even if they do not coincide with your needs."

Often, my sellers have been quite disappointed in what I have told them. However, the majority of them have always appreciated the fact that I gave them the truth, whether it was something they wanted to hear or not.

"I know my property isn't overpriced. I have called a number of the salespeople who have shown it and none of them thought it was overpriced."

"Dave and Marlene, I want you to consider the relative value of people's opinions. What I think your house is worth, what other salespeople think your house is worth, and even what you think your house is worth carry little weight compared to what potential buyers active in the marketplace today think its value is. Many sellers want me to sell a property at their price. It is impossible to sell a property at the sellers' price, unless it happens to coincide with what the property is worth. All I can do is sell your property for what it is worth. Although these other salespeople felt it was not overpriced, the potential buyers who accompanied them have expressed their opinions that it was overpriced in a very emphatic way: They didn't buy it. We have to base our decision to make an adjustment on the opinions of the buyers, as theirs are the only opinions that count."

"I love my pets, and I don't see how they could be keeping my property from selling."

"Rich and Jessica, I also have a dog and I love pets, too. However, it is an undeniable fact that pets can hamper the sale of a house. Many buyers will not consider buying any house where they see a pet inside. Although I know it is inconvenient, it is very important not to have Muffy in the house when it is shown.

"An additional factor to consider is that many buyers will cross a house off the possibility list if they detect pet odor. Although it is slight, we have had a number of salespeople and prospective buyers tell us that they noticed a pet odor in the family room and in the basement. If you want to get the highest possible net out of your house, you will need to address this problem and remove it from the buyers' consideration. Let me suggest Zenith Industrial Cleaners. They specialize in removing difficult odors from all types of commercial and residential properties. For a reasonable price, they can cure this stumbling block that is keeping many of our best prospects from considering your house."

"I take offense at this marketplace feedback that says my house is not as clean as it should be. After all, I do live here."

"Chuck and Gigi, I can understand why you have taken offense to this feedback. Naturally, every house that someone is living in is, at times, in a state of disarray. However, to sell a house, it cannot be shown in a normal, lived-in condition. We again go back to the fact that houses are bought on emotion. People are more likely to fall in love with a house that is in picture-perfect condition. This takes extra effort, but to turn a buyer on, I have a list of specific recommendations regarding the condition of your property. I strongly feel you should implement these suggestions to give us the best chance of producing a quick sale at a good price."

"Let the buyers make these repairs. If I make these repairs, I am going to want to add this on to the price of the property."

"Ron and Joyce, many sellers get repairs and improvements confused. An improvement, such as finishing a basement, will usually increase the value of a parcel of property. A repair does not raise the value of a property. All a repair does is help bring the property up to its highest possible sales price. Unfinished repairs dramatically reduce what a buyer will pay for a property. In fact, buyers commonly deduct far more than a repair will cost to complete when they are arriving at the price they will pay for the property. Unless you are working with an investor or a bargain hunter looking for a fixer-upper, most buyers expect everything to be in good working order. Only by having all of the mechanical, structural and cosmetic aspects of your house in good working order and/or acceptable condition, will you be able to achieve a sale at the optimum net."

"I do not understand why I should have to sell my house for less just because it is one of the six houses in this subdivision that back up to the railroad tracks."

"Debra and Gary, I want you to think back to when you bought this house. You got a pretty good buy, didn't you?" "Yes, we did." "Come on now, you feel like you got one hell of a good buy, don't you?" "Yes, we think we did real well." "The reason you did so well is because the railroad tracks are in the back yard. You bought your house at a discount. You bought your house at a discount because the property has what an appraiser would call 'locational depreciation.' The railroad tracks are still here. It is a main line and the trains come through here like clockwork. You bought it at a discount and the problem is still here. You are going to have to sell it at a discount."

"I know the foundation is defective. However, this house is not worth putting $3,000 in to correct this significant problem."

"I agree with you. In a house in this area and in this condition, it does not make sense to repair the foundation for $3,000, because you will not be able to get that back when the property is sold. However, I want you to consider that buyers are not going to overlook any significant defects in a property. Without question, this is a significant defect. We must reflect this in the asking price or we will not be able to generate offers."

"You want me to do all of these repairs and make all of these improvements and reduce the price? I don't see you volunteering to reduce the commission to help out."

"You are correct, I am not. Reducing the commission you pay a broker reduces the chances of your selling the house. There is less money for the broker to use for advertising the property. There is less incentive for the broker to promote and show the property if working for less. Reducing my commission would decrease the chances of your property selling. We are having enough problems trying to generate an offer. I would hate to add another one."

"A buyer wants to buy this house with FHA or VA financing. I do not see why I should have to pay the points."

"Fran and Red, you do not have to do anything, but if you do want to sell this house, we are going to have to offer financing competitive with similar properties on the market. Buyers can buy any house in the entire city they can afford. You have to find buyers for this specific house. I suggested at the time we put the property on the market that you offer FHA and VA terms, but I agreed to try marketing the house for a period of time without offering those terms. As I expected, we ran into strong resistance from the best buying prospects who considered this house. More than 60 percent of the properties sold in this price range in this part of the city are selling with FHA and VA terms. By refusing to offer these terms, you are eliminating about two-thirds of the buyers. In effect, it is going to take three times longer to sell your property. As I showed you on the discount point explanation sheet when I listed the property, if you do find conventional buyers, it is likely they will offer less than FHA or VA buyers because of the leverage they have" (see chapter 5).

"We want you to sell the property but we don't want to put a sign up because we don't want our neighbors to know our property is for sale."

"Sam and Bridget, whether you want your neighbors to know this property is for sale or not, not placing a sign in your yard won't keep them from finding out. Within a week or two, all of the salespeople from my office will be touring the property. It is inevitable someone in the neighborhood is going to notice 30 or 40 real estate salespeople going in and out of your house. Although we do not have signs on our cars, we are part of the multiple-listing service, and many companies we cooperate with have real estate signs on their cars. On top of this, there will be showings, and the neighbors are going to see the house being shown. I would like you to reconsider. Signs are one of the most effective ways of generating buyers. People who want to live in a specific neighborhood, area or subdivision, frequently drive through these areas specifically looking for signs. As many as a fourth of the houses are sold off of signs in some areas. You are severely hampering my efforts to market the property by not allowing me to put up a sign."

"I do not want you to put up a lockbox."

"I understand your concern, since there are thousands of real estate salespeople who have the same lockbox key and will have access to your house. I would like you to consider a number of things before you refuse a lockbox. The first one is that in selling hundreds of properties over a number of years, I have never had a problem with any theft or vandalism resulting from the use of a lockbox. Real estate salespeople have far more to lose than they have to gain by committing a petty theft. Also, our local board requires a hefty deposit from every salesperson before issuing a lockbox key. A few simple safeguards like putting your jewelry in a safe deposit box and not leaving cash around the house will make you feel better about the fact that there are a number of people with access to your house.

"We cannot sell your house unless we have buyers looking at it. Naturally, a series of interruptions to your normal routine will occur. The very nature of selling a house you are still occupying entails inconveniences. You can ease them by allowing us to put up a lockbox, giving us freer access to your property. What I would like to propose is this: Every time we have a potential buyer, we will arrange an appointment. However, if you are not at home and we cannot contact you otherwise, we would like permission to show the house and leave a card. There is a potential for a few surprises here. However, we instruct all showing salespeople to ring the bell and knock a number of times before showing the house, even if there is a prearranged appointment and the property is supposed to be empty.

"Another factor I want you to consider is what I call buyer psychology. Unless we have a lockbox, it is going to be difficult for us to show the property, unless you are here to open the door. It is tougher to sell a property when the sellers are in the house when it is being shown. To get top dollar, we must get the buyers to envision the property as 'their house.' We have to get them to mentally move in. The longer we can keep them in the house, the better the chance they are going to buy it. The more we can get them to poke around in the closets and cabinets, look in the attic, check out the basement for leakage and, in effect, 'test-drive' the house, the better chance we have of selling it. It is almost impossible to get buyers to 'test-drive' a house if the sellers are watching them.

"The last thing I would like you to consider is that when sellers and buyers meet, the buyers will frequently ask 'fishing' questions, such as 'Will you throw in the refrigerator if I buy the house today?' Sellers, at times, give away things they do not need to in an overanxious moment to sell the house. Whether you will or will not leave the refrigerator is not going to decide whether the prospects are going to buy this house. Salespeople act as buffers and can usually make fewer concessions without losing the buyers than the sellers can."

"We have a problem with the basement leaking. However, we have put in new paneling and carpeting and we do not want you to tell the buyer about the leakage."

This one is simple. Whenever a seller asks you to do anything illegal or unethical, you are to turn down the listing.

"Mark and Misty, I know you are fearful you are going to have a larger problem selling the house or that you will have to sell it for less if the buyers know the basement leaks. However, I cannot and will not take a listing and hide any important factors from the buyers. We have two choices here. You will either have to allow me to make full disclosure to all buying prospects or I will have to turn the listing down. I hope you understand." In most cases, your sellers will agree to the full disclosure, as this type of request falls into the "let's try it and see what happens" category.

"If I offer FHA and VA terms, I am afraid I will get a low appraisal or one that requires extensive repairs."

"Bill and Wanda, you are fully protected by the FHA or VA Escape Clause. These are required clauses in the purchase agreement of every FHA or VA sale. The clauses state that if the property does not appraise for the agreed-upon price, either side can nullify the contract without penalty. By offering FHA and VA terms, you are opening the house to a much larger pool of potential buyers, while your risk is kept under control by the FHA or VA Escape Clause.

Chapter Summary

All salespeople try to list properties "right" at the time they originally go on the market. Within a short period of time, usually within five weeks, the marketplace tells us if the original price, terms and condition are "right" or not. If not, it is our job to obtain the adjustments necessary to get the job done: to set the stage for future adjustments at the listing presentation. Adjusting to marketplace feedback is a continuous process that starts once we are on the market and ends only when a sale is pending.

9

Qualifying Buyers

This chapter contains the information necessary for basic qualifying of FHA 203B loans and fixed rate VA guaranteed loans. For other types of government insured or guaranteed loans or for unusual circumstances, you will need to obtain assistance from a loan officer as described in chapter 14.

VA GUARANTEED LOANS

VA guaranteed financing has allowed countless Americans to buy houses who could not otherwise meet the qualifications. The availability of "VA Guaranteed Loans" provides the real estate industry with a way to finance low- to middle-price-range housing. A good working knowledge of this type of financing and a willingness to work with it can significantly increase a real estate salesperson's income. Let's look at how it works.

Eligibility Requirements

The following veterans qualify for VA guaranteed financing:

1. Any veteran with a minimum of 90 days' active duty during World War II (September 16, 1940, through July 25, 1947)
2. Any veteran with 90 days' active duty during the Korean war (June 27, 1950, through July 31, 1955)
3. Any veteran with 90 days' active duty during the Vietnam war (August 5, 1964, through May 7, 1975)
4. Any veteran with 181 days of active duty during any other time period

There are no expiration dates on VA eligibility. Active duty for training purposes is not considered eligible time for a VA loan but may be used for FHA/VA benefits. In addition, prospective VA borrowers with undesirable discharges can submit their credentials for special consideration.

Veterans with questions regarding their eligibility status can contact their VA regional office to determine if and how much eligibility they are entitled to. To obtain a certificate of eligibility, veterans must have a statement of service if still in the military or their DD-214 form if they had been discharged. Their certificate can be obtained by submitting VA Form 26-1880, Request for Determination of Eligibility and Available Loan Guaranty Entitlement. These forms are available from most lenders or any VA regional office. A lender or the veteran can prepare and submit the form for processing.

Maximum VA Mortgage Amounts

Veterans may borrow up to four times their eligibility and still finance up to 100 percent of the purchase price. Current full VA entitlement was raised to $36,000 in 1988. This means the maximum VA mortgage in most areas is $110,000 ($27,500 × 4). A veteran may pay more than $110,000 for a property and obtain a VA guaranteed loan. However, the difference must be made up in cash by the VA borrower.

Maximum Borrowing Guidelines

The VA now uses a debt/income ratio for loan qualification purposes. The ratio is determined by adding the PITI (principal, interest, taxes, insurance) payment, other fixed housing costs, such as condo fees and all other long-term obligations (those obligations with fixed payments with more than six months' payments still due). The total of these debts is divided by monthly gross income (salary, other earnings, plus any other steady income). Round the ratio up to the nearest whole percentage. If the ratio is more than 41 percent, the chances are good the loan will be rejected.

The following are the monthly obligations and total housing expenses, which should not exceed 41 percent of gross monthly income:

- Principal, interest, taxes and insurance
- Long-term debts (6 months or more)
- Child-care and/or child-support expense
- Condo/association fees
- Alimony

Notes on Discount Points

When using a VA guarantee, the buyer is not allowed to pay any portion of the discount points. Points may be paid by the seller or any third party other than the seller.

Additional Benefits of VA Financing

There is no limit to the number of VA guaranteed loans a veteran may obtain. An entitlement may be used more than once as long as previously guaranteed loans taken out by the veteran are either paid off in full or if the veteran obtained a "substitution of entitlement" from a qualified veteran buyer on a loan assumption sale. In some instances, veterans can obtain additional VA guaranteed loans even if previously guaranteed loans are not paid off or released *if* the veterans did not use all of their eligibility to obtain previous loans *and* if they have enough remaining eligibility to qualify for a subsequent loan.

Another real advantage is the ability of a veteran to use VA financing to buy up to a four-unit residential building as long as the veteran occupies one of the units.

FHA INSURED MORTGAGES

Contrary to popular belief, the FHA does not make loans. They insure qualified lending institutions that the buyer of the loan is good, and, if the buyer defaults, the FHA will provide remedies to protect the lender.

The most commonly used FHA loan is an FHA 203B. This loan is available to anyone buying a personal residence who has acceptable credit and adequate income as determined by FHA underwriting guidelines. This type of loan offers many advantages. With the exception of VA guaranteed loans, it provides the highest loan to value mortgage ratio available, allowing the buyer to buy a house with very little money down. With the exception of one FHA program, the interest rates are fixed and usually lower than the going conventional rate. There is no prepayment penalty on FHA loans and they are freely assumable. (Please note that FHA loans that originated after December 1, 1986, do have some restrictions on their assumability in the first two years of the life of the loan.)

Determining the FHA Maximum Mortgage

When using what is called the acquisition method, the buyers may add their nonrecurring closing costs to the loan. The sales price plus the closing costs as allowed by the FHA (see Form 9-1) give you what is called the acquisition cost. The down payment for properties where the acquisition cost is $50,000 or less is three percent of the acquisition cost. For properties where the acquisition cost exceeds $50,000, the down payment is three percent of the first $25,000 and five percent on the amount of acquisition cost over $25,000.

In addition to allowing the buyers to put their nonrecurring closing costs on the loan, the FHA allows the buyers the option of adding the FHA Mortgage Insurance Premium (MIP) onto the loan. The MIP, when financed, varies from 2.4 percent of the loan amount to 3.8 percent of the loan amount, depending on the length of amortization of the loan (see Form 9.2). The Mortgage Insurance Premium is a onetime fee that most buyers do add to the loan rather than pay it in cash.

FHA Qualifying Guidelines

The FHA has a standard qualifying process that is outlined on Form 9-3. It starts with the potential borrowers' gross monthly income. You then deduct their Federal Income Tax (see Form 9-4A and 9-4B) to give you the borrowers' net monthly income. You then must calculate the principle, interest, taxes and insurance, and association fee, if any, plus the maintenance and utilities on the house they are buying. These figures together give you your total housing expense. The total housing expense should not exceed 38 percent of net monthly income. The next step is to add the total housing expense with all the other fixed expenses the borrowers will incur on a monthly basis. The total of the housing expense and other fixed expenses should not exceed 53 percent of the net monthly income.

Chapter Summary

The information in this chapter gives you a basic understanding of how FHA and VA loans work. For difficult qualification situations, you should rely on the advice of a competent loan officer to counsel the prospective buyers and match them with the right financing package for their needs.

Form 9-1   Determining FHA Maximum Mortgage

I a. Sales Price $_____
   b. Plus FHA estimate of closing costs*   +_____
      *If seller pays any portion of buyers' closing
      costs, add "0."
   c. Acquisition Cost   =_____

II a. (1) For acquisition cost up to $50,000— $_____
      97 percent of first $50,000
      (2) For acquisition cost exceeding $_____
      $50,000—97 percent of first $25,000, 95
      percent of balance over $25,000 up to ac-
      quisition cost of statutory limit, whichever is
      less
   b. Maximum Mortgage—Pre-MIP   =_____
      (rounded down to $50 increment)*
      *Loan origination fee is based on this
      amount.
   c. For Nonowner Occupied Property: Maxi-
      mum mortgage is 85 percent of acquisition
      or statutory limit, whichever is less.

III a. Sales Price $_____
    b. Less Maximum Mortgage (no MIP)   −_____
    c. Minimum Down Payment   =_____

IV a. Maximum Mortgage (no MIP) $_____
    b. Multiplied by MIP factor   ×_____
    c. Total MIP   =_____

V a. Maximum Mortgage (no MIP) $_____
   b. Plus MIP financed (total MIP rounded down +_____
      to next $50 increment)
   c. New FHA Mortgage   =_____

VI a. Total MIP $_____
    b. Less MIP added to Mortgage   −_____
    c. Amount of MIP buyers need to pay at clos-
       ing   =_____

Form 9-2   Onetime MIP Factor Table

Portion of MIP Financed	Repayment Term in Years			
	Less than 18	18–22	23–25	Over 25
100%	.02400	.03000	.03600	.03800
0%	.02344	.02913	.03475	.03661

FHA Estimated Closing Costs

Sales Price	Closing Costs	Sales Price	Closing Costs
$10,000–12,999	$ 450	$ 64,000– 68,999	$1,100
13,000–16,999	500	69,000– 72,999	1,150
17,000–21,999	550	73,000– 78,999	1,200
22,000–26,999	600	79,000– 81,999	1,250
27,000–29,999	650	82,000– 85,999	1,300
30,000–33,999	700	86,000– 89,999	1,350
34,000–38,999	750	90,000– 94,999	1,400
39,000–42,999	800	95,000– 98,999	1,450
43,000–46,999	850	99,000–103,999	1,500
47,000–50,999	900	104,000–107,999	1,550
51,000–55,999	950	108,000–112,999	1,600
56,000–59,999	1,000	113,000–116,999	1,650
60,000–63,999	1,050	117,000–121,999	1,700
		122,000–	1,750

Form 9-3   FHA Qualifying Guide

A. Total Gross Income $ _____
B. Subtract Federal Tax (see tables) – _____
C. Net Monthly Income = $ _____
D. P.I.T.I. and association fee (if any) $ _____
E. Maintenance and Utilities (avg. $165) + _____
F. Total Housing Expense (D + E) = $ _____
   *Divide F by C
   (Maximum 38 percent) _____percent
G. State Income Tax $ + _____
H. Social Security (.0751 x each gross income) + _____
I. Monthly Payments + _____
J. Monthly Child-Care Expense + _____
K. Total Housing Expense (Line F) + _____
L. Total Fixed Payments (Add lines G-K) = $ _____
   *Divide L by C
   (Maximum 53 percent) _____percent

Form 9-4A   MARRIED Persons—
MONTHLY Payroll Period

(For Wages Paid After December 1987)

And the wages are—		And the number of witholding allowances claimed is—							
		0	1	2	3	4	5	6	7
At least	But less than	The amount of income tax to be withheld shall be—							
$1,320	$1,360	$163	$139	$114	$ 90	$65	$ 41	$ 17	$ 0
1,360	1,400	169	145	120	96	71	47	23	0
1,400	1,440	175	151	126	102	77	53	29	4
1,440	1,480	181	157	132	108	83	59	35	10
1,480	1,520	187	163	138	114	89	65	41	16
1,520	1,560	193	169	144	120	95	71	47	22
1,560	1,600	199	175	150	126	101	71	53	28
1,600	1,640	205	181	156	132	107	83	59	34
1,640	1,680	211	187	162	138	113	89	65	40
1,680	1,720	217	193	168	144	119	95	71	46
1,720	1,760	223	199	174	150	125	101	77	52
1,760	1,800	229	205	180	156	131	107	83	58
1,800	1,840	235	211	186	162	137	113	89	64
1,840	1,880	241	217	192	168	143	119	95	70
1,880	1,920	247	223	198	174	149	125	101	76
1,920	1,960	253	229	204	180	155	131	107	82
1,960	2,000	259	235	210	186	161	137	113	88
2,000	2,040	265	241	216	192	167	143	119	94
2,040	2,080	271	247	222	198	173	149	125	100
2,080	2,120	277	253	228	204	179	155	131	106
2,120	2,160	283	259	234	210	185	161	137	112
2,160	1,200	289	265	240	216	191	167	143	118
2,200	2,240	295	271	246	222	197	173	149	124
2,240	2,280	301	277	252	228	203	179	155	130
2,280	2,320	307	283	258	234	209	185	161	136
2,320	2,360	313	289	264	240	215	191	167	142
2,360	2,400	319	295	270	246	221	197	173	148
2,400	2,440	325	301	276	252	227	203	179	154
2,440	2,480	331	307	282	258	233	209	185	160
2,480	2,520	337	313	288	264	239	215	191	166
2,520	2,560	343	319	294	270	245	221	197	172
2,560	2,600	349	325	300	276	251	227	203	178
2,600	2,640	355	331	306	282	257	233	209	184
2,640	2,680	361	337	312	288	263	239	215	190
2,680	2,720	367	343	318	294	269	245	221	196

2,720	2,760	374	349	324	300	275	251	227	202
2,760	2,800	385	355	330	306	281	257	233	208
2,800	2,840	396	361	336	312	287	263	239	214
2,840	2,880	407	367	342	318	293	269	245	220
2,880	2,920	419	373	348	324	299	275	251	226
2,920	2,960	430	394	354	330	305	281	257	232
2,960	3,000	441	395	360	336	311	287	263	238
3,000	3,040	452	407	366	342	317	293	269	244
3,040	3,080	463	418	372	348	323	299	275	250
3,080	3,120	475	429	384	354	329	305	281	256
3,120	3,160	486	440	395	360	335	311	287	262
3,160	3,200	497	451	406	366	341	317	293	268
3,200	3,240	508	463	417	372	347	323	299	274
3,240	3,280	519	474	428	383	353	329	305	280
3,280	3,320	531	485	440	394	359	335	311	286
3,320	3,360	542	496	451	405	365	341	317	292
3,360	3,400	553	507	462	416	371	347	323	298
3,400	3,440	564	519	473	428	382	353	329	304
3,440	3,480	575	530	484	439	393	359	335	310
3,480	3,520	587	541	496	450	405	365	541	316
3,520	3,560	598	552	507	461	416	371	347	322
3,560	3,600	609	563	518	472	427	381	353	328
3,600	3,640	620	575	529	484	438	393	359	334
3,640	3.680	631	586	540	495	449	404	365	340
3,680	3,720	643	597	552	506	461	415	371	346
3,720	3,760	654	608	563	517	472	426	381	352
3,760	3.800	665	619	574	528	483	437	392	358
3,800	3,840	676	631	585	540	494	449	403	364
3,840	3,880	687	642	596	551	505	460	414	370
3,880	3,920	699	653	608	562	527	471	426	380

$5,200 and over   Use Table 4(b) for a MARRIED person

(b) MARRIED person

If the amount
(after subtracting   *The amount of income tax*
withholding allowances) is: *to be withheld shall be:*

Not over $254 0

Over—	*But not over—*		*of excess over—*
$254	*—$2,733*	*15%*	*—$254*
$2,733	*—$6,246*	*$371.88 plus 28%*	*—$2,733*
$6,246	*—$15,422*	*$1,355.38 plus 33%*	*—$6,246*
$15,422	. . . .	*$4,383.40 plus 28%*	*—$15,422*

Form 9-4B   SINGLE Persons—MONTHLY Payroll Period

(For Wages Paid After December 1987)

And the wages are—		And the number of witholding allowances claimed is—							
		0	1	2	3	4	5	6	7
At least	But less than	The amount of income tax to be withheld shall be—							
$ 440	$ 460	$ 54	$ 30	$ 6	$ 0	$ 0	$ 0	$ 0	$ 0
460	480	57	33	9	0	0	0	0	0
480	500	60	36	12	0	0	0	0	0
500	520	63	39	15	0	0	0	0	0
520	540	66	42	18	0	0	0	0	0
540	560	69	45	21	0	0	0	0	0
560	580	72	48	24	0	0	0	0	0
580	600	75	51	27	2	0	0	0	0
600	640	80	56	31	7	0	0	0	0
640	680	86	62	37	13	0	0	0	0
680	720	92	68	43	19	0	0	0	0
720	760	98	74	49	25	0	0	0	0
760	800	104	80	55	31	6	0	0	0
800	840	110	86	61	37	12	0	0	0
840	880	116	92	67	43	18	0	0	0
880	920	122	98	73	49	24	0	0	0
920	960	128	104	79	55	30	6	0	0
960	1,000	133	109	86	62	38	15	0	0
1,000	1,040	140	116	91	67	42	18	0	0
1,040	1,080	146	122	97	73	48	24	0	0
1,080	1,120	152	128	103	79	54	30	6	0
1,120	1,160	158	134	109	85	60	36	12	0
1,160	1,200	164	140	115	91	66	42	18	0
1,200	1,240	170	146	121	97	72	48	24	0
1,240	1,280	176	152	127	103	78	54	30	5
1,280	1,320	182	158	133	109	84	60	36	11
1,320	1,360	188	164	139	115	90	66	42	17
1,360	1,400	194	170	145	121	96	72	48	23
1,400	1,440	200	176	151	127	102	78	54	29
1,440	1,480	206	182	157	133	108	84	60	35
1,480	1,520	212	188	163	139	114	90	66	41
1,520	1,560	218	194	169	145	120	96	72	47
1,560	1,600	225	200	175	151	126	102	78	53
1,600	1,640	236	206	181	157	132	108	84	59
1,640	1,680	247	212	187	163	138	114	90	65

1,680	1,720	258	218	193	169	144	120	96	71
1,720	1,760	269	224	199	175	150	126	102	77
1,760	1,800	281	235	205	181	156	132	108	83
1,800	1,840	292	246	211	187	162	138	114	89
1,840	1,880	303	257	217	193	168	144	120	95
1,880	1,920	314	269	223	199	174	150	126	101
1,920	1,960	325	280	234	205	180	156	132	107
1,960	2,000	337	291	246	211	186	162	138	113
2,000	2,040	348	302	257	217	192	168	144	119
2,040	2,080	359	313	268	223	198	174	150	125
2,080	2,120	370	325	279	234	204	180	156	131
2,120	2,160	381	336	290	245	210	186	162	137
2,160	2,200	393	347	302	256	216	192	168	143
2,200	2,240	404	358	313	267	222	198	174	149
2,240	2,280	415	369	324	278	233	204	180	155
2,280	2,320	426	381	335	290	244	210	186	161
2,320	2,360	437	392	346	301	255	216	192	167
2,360	2,400	449	403	358	312	267	222	198	173
2,400	2,440	460	414	369	323	278	232	204	179
2,440	2,480	471	425	380	334	289	243	210	185
2,480	2,520	482	437	391	346	300	255	216	191
2,520	2,560	493	448	402	357	311	266	222	197
2,560	2,600	505	459	414	368	323	277	232	203
2,600	2,640	516	470	425	379	334	288	243	209
2,640	2,680	527	481	436	390	345	299	254	215
2,680	2,720	538	493	447	402	356	311	265	221
2,720	2,760	549	504	458	413	367	322	276	231
2,760	2,800	561	515	470	424	379	333	288	242
2,800	2,840	572	526	481	435	390	344	299	253
2,840	2,880	583	537	492	446	401	355	310	264

$4,240 and over   Use Table 4(a) for a SINGLE person

(a) SINGLE person—including head of household:

If the amount of wages (after subtracting withholding allowances) is:	The amount of income tax to be withheld shall be:

Not over $88 .0

Over—	But not over—		of excess over—
$88	—$1,575	15%	—$88
$1,575	—$3,683	$223.13 plus 28%	—$1,575
$3,683	—$8,461	$813.46 plus 33%	—$3,683
$8,461	. . . .	$2,390.03 plus 28%	—$8,461

10

Writing Offers

Qualifying the buyers by completing the *U*, *E* and *S* of QUEST as outlined in chapter 3 will set the stage for writing the offer. A number of the basic closes outlined in chapter 4, such as "The Foundation Close," "The Write-Them-Up Close," "The Ask-for-the-Order/Tie-Down Close," "The Original Motivation Close" and "The Urgency Close" are all excellent in preparing the buyers to submit an offer. The objections in this chapter are typical of what the selling salesperson encounters when writing the original offer. Learning to close on these objections will not only get your buyers "on paper" at the earliest possible time but will also allow you to write the best offer possible the first time around.

"I want to write a ridiculous offer."

Buyers commonly want to start written negotiations by making a ridiculous offer. By their very nature, buyers want to negotiate the asking price, the terms or the condition of the property. Unfortunately, by making too low or too ridiculous of an initial offer, the buyers frequently alienate the sellers, thus souring the negotiations. All sellers have a price under which they feel any offers are an insult. Because of this, the buyers' best strategy is to make an offer that is low enough to make the sellers wince and say, "Ooh, that is just a little less than we wanted to go," but not so low that the sellers look at it and say, "This guy is some kind of thief, trying to steal my property. To heck with him. Let's counter at the full price."

Keep in mind that in most cases you represent the sellers, and your job is to get the best price possible for the sellers. So although the above strategy is in the best interests of the buyers, introducing this thought is not always working against the best interests of the sellers. After all, if we do not get the buyers to make an original offer, no matter what their motivation, we have *no* chance of working out an acceptable sale for our sellers.

An effective dialogue to use with your buyers may go like this: "Fred and Barbara, this property is listed at $114,000. You want to make an offer for less. Your best chance of obtaining this property, and you do want this property, is to make a full-price offer. If I cannot get you to make a full-price offer, I would like you to consider offering the highest price you would consider paying for the property. Many buyers assume that if they make a really low offer, they will find out if the sellers will give the house away, or they will find out how badly these sellers want out of the house. Unfortunately, a ridiculous offer alienates and frequently angers the sellers, destroying your negotiating position. Your chances of getting the sellers to make the concessions you seek is by making an offer that could be considered hard bargaining on the part of the sellers, but not so low as to be considered ridiculous. Offers considered to be an insult by the sellers commonly make them stiffen in their resolve to get the "asking price"! The effectiveness of all your other negotiating tools are diminished once you have angered the sellers. In addition, you could lose this house by making a less-than-solid offer if another buyer happens to submit an offer today that is more realistic. The odds on this are slight, but I have seen it happen. Let's increase your chances of buying this property by starting the negotiations in a reasonable way."

"Let's split the difference."

Once an initial offer is made, the buyers or sellers may want to "split the difference." This approach is valid only as long as the buyers and sellers are an equal distance from a reasonable price on the property. Say the property is listed for $90,000, with a fair market value of $85,000. Our buyers make an $80,000 offer. Splitting the difference would be a reasonable and feasible way to approach this particular situation. However, what if the property is priced at $90,000 and is worth $85,000 and the buyers make an offer for $85,000? Your sellers want to split the difference. The market data indicates that $85,000 is an excellent offer, and it is an offer our sellers should take. Splitting the difference would likely end up in losing the sale.

We can split the difference into infinity and never reach an agreement. Splitting the difference when the buyers and sellers are close will frequently break negotiations at the very time we should have an accepted contract in our hands. *Only "split the difference" when the buyers and sellers are equidistant from a fair settlement.*

"We like the basic house, location and offering terms, but, boy, does this place need work! This house needs more done to it than we really want to do. We are not looking for a fixer-upper."

In today's marketplace, many buyers expect a house to be in good condition before they will buy it. Unless you are in a red-hot sellers' market, buyers have a wide variety of homes to pick from and need to be persuaded to consider a property that needs work. There are two basic ways to convince the buyers to buy a neglected property. Try the following:

"Jim and Ginny, I have two suggestions to remedy this problem. If condition problems are the only reason you do not want to buy this house, let's ask the sellers to do the following work you feel needs to be done, whether it is cleaning, replacing carpeting, painting rooms or making repairs. If you are uncomfortable with letting them do this work, we can build an allowance into the sale for whatever you feel the improvements are worth, whether it be $1,000, $1,500 or $2,000. We can then write up the sale so this work will be done by the people you choose and will be paid out of the sellers' proceeds in the agreed-upon amount.

"Another alternative is to reduce your offer by the amount you feel the work will cost. You are planning on putting down a substantial down payment. It is possible to lessen the down payment and still make this sale work. How about this? Hold back $2,000 of your down payment, buy the house for $2,000 less and have the work done with the money you held back. Condition is one of the most easily corrected problems in buying a house. We obviously cannot do anything with location, and there is a limited amount we can do with terms. Condition problems are fairly easy to correct, and I would hate to see you miss buying the 'right house' just because of needed cosmetic repairs.

"Another factor to consider is what I refer to as the 'one-in-four rule.' Generally speaking, for every dollar in cosmetic repairs a property needs, there is a corresponding drop of about four dollars in the market value. In plain words, a house that should sell for approximately $60,000 that needs $1,000 worth of paint and carpeting may sell for as little as $56,000. Part of that one-for-four reduction has already been reflected in the lower asking price of the house. If you buy this house and are willing to make that $1 investment for every $4 you save on the purchase price, you can get quite a lot more house for your money. If you have the skills to do the painting or carpet replacement yourself, the savings can be even greater. This will allow you to get more house than you would normally be able to buy and still keep your payments within reason.

"Another plus we have not considered is that if you are going to paint and recarpet, you can personalize the house and redecorate it to your own tastes. You will not be stuck with somebody else's carpet color or paint scheme. You can paint and carpet to your own likes at a very reasonable price."

"Well, if they do not want to accept our offer, let's let them sit for a week and soften up and then resubmit our offer and see what they think."

This sentiment is frequently expressed when a buyers' original offer is countered by the sellers'. There are two basic approaches.

"Don and Marlene, I understand your disappointment in receiving a counteroffer. However, I sense that you did not think your original offer would be accepted in the first place. Admittedly, there was quite a bit of wishing and hoping built into that offer.

"You have been looking at properties for some time, haven't you? This is the first house that really fits your wants and needs that you can comfortably afford. You certainly have the right to wait a week. However, this house may be gone in a week. It is a good buy. If it wasn't, you would not have made your original offer. I would hate to see you lose the house you really want in an effort to get it for less than it is worth. Consider the situation in this light: Would you be disappointed if you received a call from me tomorrow, telling you the house was sold to another buyer? If you would be, the time to buy this house is today and not next week."

If that doesn't do the trick, try this: "There is one other factor I want you to consider before deciding to wait a week and resubmitting your offer. In most cases, when buyers make the sellers wait for a response, the sellers become firm in their resolve to obtain the original listed price. When asked to wait around after receiving the same offer a week later, some sellers come back with an even worse counteroffer than they did in the first place. They feel the buyers are game playing. Their attitude is, if the buyers are going to play the negotiating game that way, we are going to resort to the same tactics. Let's not lose this sale by employing negotiating tactics that are unlikely to help you."

"I do not see why I should make an earnest deposit as big as you are suggesting. I just want to make a $500 earnest deposit." Earnest deposits are the glue that holds sales together. The larger the earnest deposit, the better. It is not earnest unless the buyer becomes short of breath at the thought of losing the money.

Obtaining a large earnest deposit is actually one of the easier things we do. In almost every case the buyers want to negotiate price, terms or condition. When buyers suggest or insist on writing an offer of less than the listing price, you can use the following approach:

"Chris and Kathy, the smaller the earnest deposit you make, the more you decrease your leverage in trying to negotiate other points of this agreement. You want to write an offer at less than the listed price. I am sure you would like to get this offer accepted. I want to explain one of the secrets of getting low offers accepted, a secret that will increase your chances of getting this offer accepted without a counter, a secret that will allow you to do this and will not cost you any more money. The secret is simple: *Make a large earnest deposit.* By making a large earnest deposit, you can convince the sellers you are serious about buying the house. Only by making a large earnest deposit are the sellers confident that you are serious buyers. That is their insurance that you are serious about following through with the closing. Small earnest deposits are like waving a red flag in front of a bull when talking to sellers. They see all risk and no gain. They are taking their house off the market for weeks and possibly months. Their only protection if the buyers back out is the earnest deposit. I would advise you to make an earnest deposit of no less than $7,500."

How big should the earnest deposit be? Although each type of loan requires a down payment of different sizes, always ask for at least ten percent of the sales price if at least that much will have to be produced in cash by the buyer at closing. If they do not need that much, ask for all the money they are going to need to close, as follows:

"Chris and Kathy, you can buy this house with a relatively small down payment. Your total down payment, closing costs and prepaids are going to be approximately $8,500. To maximize the chances of getting this contract accepted, I suggest you make an earnest deposit of $8,500."

They may look shocked, but you will get a much larger earnest deposit than if you had started out asking for $1,000. Get the maximum number of sales closed by following this rule: *Negotiate for the largest possible earnest deposit to ensure the closing.*

"We want to think about it. Dad was a pretty good negotiator, and he always said you should sleep on a big decision before making it."

"Chris and Kathy, I understand your reluctance to make a decision this big. This is a major decision for you and you want to make sure you move correctly. However, your desire to wait until tomorrow to make a decision tells me a number of things. It tells me there is something I have not fully explained to you. There is still an unanswered question keeping you from making a decision. Before we part, I would like to know all the reasons keeping you from making your decision. If you wait until you are home to voice your concerns, I will not be there to explain them, whether they are regarding financing, obtaining a clear title, length of the loan processing, closing date, possession date and so forth. I am here now to answer any questions you have, and I would like to get all of the contributing factors resolved or negotiated before you go home." Once you have resolved all of their questions and concerns, there is no point to wait until tomorrow, and that is the thrust of this technique.

Another approach to use when they want to sleep on it is to explain to them the following: "I want you to consider the fact that the human mind, although capable of remembering a lot, has to process thousands of images, facts, advertising messages and so forth every day. Today, we have covered dozens of points about the potential purchase of this house. It has been said that the human mind will retain only half of what it is exposed to for 24 hours. By tomorrow it is likely you will forget a number of important things we discussed today. Rather than sleeping on it, I think you are better off making a decision while this is fresh in your mind. I would like you to isolate why you feel the need to wait until tomorrow. If we can recognize and resolve your concerns, we should be able to make a decision today."

"We like them both and cannot make a decision." At times you will have the pleasant problem of narrowing the buying prospects down to two houses, one that the husband likes and one that the wife prefers. It is a matter of making a decision between the two. The best way to resolve this is to use the "Ben Franklin Close" as outlined in chapter 4. Draw a line down the middle of a plain sheet of paper and put the pluses and minuses of each house on each side of the line.

If it is apparent that one of the two parties is the decision maker and in firm control, arrange things so the decision maker has your help in convincing the spouse. You can do this by saying, "I think you need a little time to talk about this between yourselves. I'll go into a conference room, and you two can stay here in my office to discuss the two houses. Call on me to answer any questions."

"Just about everything is right with this house except it is just too far from work." Prospective buyer: "I currently live in the Field Club area, and it is only ten minutes to downtown. This is at least another five miles from downtown, and I don't know if I want to drive that much extra every day." This particular objection can be countered in a number of ways, and this alone is not a reason to not buy the house. The first approach is to convert distance to time.

"Fred, you are correct. This is approximately five miles farther from downtown than the Field Club area. I do not want you to think of it in terms of five miles though. My husband works downtown, and we also live in this area. As you said, Field Club is only ten minutes from downtown. My husband has found that if he goes east on Highway 66 and turns north on 13th Street, he can be downtown and have his car parked in 17 minutes. Although this is approximately five miles farther from downtown, it's only seven minutes farther in time. I think you will agree that seven minutes a day is not a reason to not live in the neighborhood you like.

"There are a number of other factors I would like you to consider. There is a correlation between how close you want to be to work and the price of houses. By making a seven-minute-longer commute, you can save yourself approximately ten percent in the purchase price of your home. There is a corresponding drop in monthly payments of ten percent also. This is quite a saving compared to the extra cost of seven minutes a day when driving to work. Not only are the prices less expensive the farther you get away from the downtown business district, the taxes are lower also. This is again reflected in lower payments.

"Another consideration is the added enjoyment that comes from living in the style of home and location you really wanted. The amenities in this neighborhood better fit the life-style of you, your wife and your children than the area you are in right now." Sell the amenities and the distance problem fades away. "The last thing I would like you to consider is the size of the lots and the fact that this area is not as heavily developed. The concentration of population is not as great here. Although it's not quite like living in the country in the city, it is a much more countrylike atmosphere than your current neighborhood."

"We really do want to buy a house, but we think we are going to wait until spring." "May I ask you why?" "We want to save more money for a down payment." "Let me ask you, Joe and Mary Fran, how much are you able to save every month?" "We are able to save about $150 a month." "Saving $150 a month adds up to $1,800 a year. You are considering buying a house in the $80,000 price range. Houses in this price range are increasing in value approximately five percent a year. That is $4,000, or about $330 a month. These houses are going up in price faster than you can save. Every month, you are losing ground to the tune of about $180. You have a large enough down payment at this time to purchase the property. I would not want to see you lose equity by putting off your decision.

"There is also the uncertainty of interest rates to consider. Rates are moderate at this time. When rates are low to moderate like they are right now, one of two things will happen: Either prices will go up because housing is more affordable or the interest rates will go up because demand is higher. Most likely, both of these things will happen. There is no better time to buy a house than right now. The longer you wait, the better the chances are you are going to be paying higher prices and a higher interest rate."

If current rates are high, use this approach: "Marv and Charlene, you are thinking of waiting until next spring when the rates will hopefully go down. The value of real estate and the resulting price you must pay is a function of interest rates. You are convinced interest rates are going down in the spring. When rates are high like they are right now, housing sales are slow, and prices are quite depressed. Because of this, there are some great buys available at this time. If rates do drop by next spring, the chances are overwhelmingly good that prices are going to start skyrocketing. You will end up paying more money for less house in your quest to get a lower interest rate.

"It is not necessary to wait for a lower rate to protect yourself. There are two things you can do. You can either get an adjustable rate mortgage, which will automatically lower the interest rate if rates drop, as you think they will. If they drop, which I think they will also, the corresponding value of your house is likely to go up, and you will have made an excellent purchase. If you are uncomfortable with an adjustable rate mortgage, you can obtain a fixed-rate mortgage, FHA or VA if possible, and refinance your loan if there is a dramatic drop in rates. As you have seen from the material I have given you, housing prices are the most reasonable they have been for some time, and the area in which you want to buy has some excellent buys. You have visited with a loan officer, and she assured us that you qualify to buy a house in this area. Consider the different options, and I believe you will find it in your best interests to buy now, while prices are low."

Try this alternative approach. "Denny and Cheryl, it is currently taking about two months to close a sale. In some instances, sellers are asking for two to four weeks' time in the house after the closing to arrange their move, close on the house they are buying and so forth. If you found the right house today, in many cases it would be three months before you actually moved in. It is now November. That means you would be moving in toward the end of February, almost March. March is springtime. Buying now with prices and rates where they are will allow you to find and buy the best house for your needs at the best price and total cost.

"Denny and Cheryl, we spent quite a bit of time together discovering your wants and needs in a house. We have looked at a number of homes and we are getting very close to finding the perfect house for you, the one house in today's market that meets your wants and needs. Let's complete the journey we have started, put this together, and by spring, you will have the moving all over. It will be behind you, you will be moved in and you will be able to get on with your life without this house purchase hanging over your head."

"We really want to buy a house but we don't have enough money down." This is a lament frequently voiced by potential buyers. Try any or all of the following:

"Bill and Rose, have you recently prepared a complete financial statement of yourselves, listing all of your assets and liabilities? Many of us are worth far more than we think. I would be willing to sit down with you and help you put one together."

Oftentimes, when making a financial statement, buyers will see that they have other assets they can tap on to come up with the money to buy a house. After completing a net worth statement, you can see if they have any hidden assets, such as bonds or cash-value life insurance they can borrow against to use as a down payment. Perhaps they have other major assets that are unencumbered that they may borrow money against to use as a down payment. Borrowing against assets to get money for a down payment on a house is perfectly okay as long as the loan is taken out before they buy the house and as long as it doesn't push their ratios over acceptable limits.

Perhaps the prospective buyers have a bonus coming up that they can get an advancement on or borrow against. In most cases, they can borrow against an income tax refund not yet received. There are numerous solutions. In less expensive houses, the buyers can use either an FHA 203B and add their closing costs and mortgage insurance to the loan, or they can use an FHA 221 D2, which allows them to buy with a very small initial investment. If the buyers are VA qualified, we can frequently ask the sellers to pay any or all of the buyers' closing costs and prepaids, get a 100 percent loan and get the buyers in for absolutely no cash outlay at all. I have had students ask me if this is a good way to sell a house. As long as the sellers net what they want to net from the house, and you can get the buyers qualified, it is an absolutely marvelous way to sell a property.

With first-time buyers, Mom and Dad are often willing to help out and a gift letter can be used. Although gift letters are restricted on some types of financing, they are still allowed on FHA and VA loans and can be employed with great effect. A gift letter is merely a letter from the parents or a relative or friend stating that they are giving the buyers the money they are going to need to close, and it will not have to be paid back.

At times, we have buyers with many small loans in different places. A number of credit cards, a small car loan here, a furniture loan there and so forth. This pushes their ratios out of shape and can keep them from qualifying for a loan. Arrange for them to visit their banker to explore the possibility of a consolidation loan. Consolidate all of these loans into one loan, stretch out the payments, get the best rate possible and frequently you can bring the ratios in line.

Ratios can be improved in a number of additional ways. It may come down to buyers selling their RV, four-wheel drive or boat with huge payments in order to qualify to buy a house. It is asking a lot of buyers to give up one part of their life-style to improve their life-style in another way. However, I have had many buyers sell their expensive "playthings," which are not necessary to their everyday life, in order to buy the house of their dreams.

Ratio problems can also be combatted by selling the buyers on the benefits of a graduated mortgage payment loan. This can be used to get buyers to qualify at up to a 20 percent higher sales price than they would on a fixed-rate loan. The use of variable or renegotiable rate mortgages will also bring the total house payment down and help when you are confronted with a tight ratio qualification.

If you have buyers who really want to buy a house and cannot buy it at this time because of ratio problems, you can suggest they get a second job. This will do two things. It will allow them to pay off some of their smaller short-term debts, such as credit cards and furniture loans, and will also, once they have been six months or so on the job, count as added income. By reducing debt and increasing income, you can get them to the point where within six months or a year they will be able to qualify for a house that meets their wants and needs.

With some types of loans, Mom and Dad or a relative or mentor can agree to be a co-signer, so your buyers can obtain the loan.

This last technique can occasionally be used when selling new homes. It is the exchange of "sweat equity" in lieu of making part or all of the down payment.

"The payments are just a little too high."

Prospective buyer: "Jim, when we first sat down, we told you we did not want to go above $800 a month. After seeing what we could buy for that amount, we said we would consider $850.

Then, after looking a little more, we said $900 a month, and no more. Now we have found the house we really want and you tell us the lowest we can get the payments is $960. We were up last night until two o'clock, lying in bed, talking about this. If we had $960 monthly payments, we could not sleep. We could not even sleep thinking about it, and we haven't bought the house yet. We are just afraid we will not be able to meet these payments."

For example, let's say these buyers are well qualified for $960 a month. In fact, our loan officer says they can qualify for up to $1,150 to $1,200 a month. They are simply nervous because it is quite a jump over their current house payment. You can use any of the following approaches:

"Harvey and Sue, your basic objection is the payments are $60 higher than you want to make. Harvey, you work downtown, and I assume you eat lunch every day. What do you spend? Say, maybe, $3 on lunch? That's $60 a month. I know you play golf on the average of once a week. Your golf has to be costing you at least $15 a week. That's $60 a month. Between lunches and golf, you spend $120 a month. That's $4 a day on the average between the two—$60 a month in the form of a higher house payment is $2 a day. Wait a minute. It's not $2 a day. You are in the 28 percent tax bracket, meaning that all of your payments in the first five years will be written off against your income taxes. This means it is not $2 a day. It is about $1.44 a day. You spend an average of $4 for lunch and golf a day, and you are *not* going to buy the house you want to buy, you are *not* going to live in the neighborhood you want to live in, and you are *not* going to send your children to the schools they want to go to all for $1.44 a day? I think if you put this $60 a month in perspective, you will agree it is not a logical reason to *not* buy this house. I do understand your fears and your not wanting to stay awake at nights worrying about the payment being $960 instead of $900, but if you look at it in the overall context of your monthly gross and net income, this $60 is a relatively small item."

Try the following when selling a new house: "I would also like you to consider a few other compensating factors. This is a new house. You are moving out of an old house, and, when I helped you sell it, I realized your utility bills were quite high. The furnace on this house is one of the newer, higher-efficiency-rated furnaces. We have triple-pane-insulated windows, and we have R36 insulation in the ceilings. Although your house payment is considerably higher, that is going to be offset somewhat by the compensating factor of lower utility bills.

"I also want you to consider this location. This is where the two of you have wanted to live for the last four years. You have both worked hard and earned promotions in your respective professions. You deserve to live here. You have earned it, and I hate to see $1.44 a day keep you from buying the house you truly want."

You can also use the following approach: "Joe and Carol, your income history has shown that every year you both get raises and your income has increased every year you have been married. This house is truly the one that best meets your wants and needs. According to lending standards and the guidelines we normally follow, you can comfortably afford this payment, although you feel it may be a little tight. Let's assume your income keeps increasing as it has every year for the last eight years. This feeling of it being just a little snug cannot last more than a year or two. Don't you feel that a year or two of maybe being a little more careful with your money in exchange for buying a house you want to buy is worth that small sacrifice?"

CLOSING THE NEW HOMEBUYER

New homes offer opportunities and benefits existing houses do not. You need to explore and explain those opportunities and benefits to your buyers to overcome the frequently higher price someone will have to pay to obtain a new home.

Prospective buyer: "This is a nice house. However, I can still buy more house for the same money if I buy an existing home."

"Yes, Mike, it is true you are paying a higher per foot cost for a new home, but I do not think you fully understand the benefits of owning a new home, benefits that more than offset this slightly higher price. This house has a warranty. It is warranted by the builder and a warranty agency for ten years against major defects. (Check what kind of warranty is normally provided by builders in your area.) You are getting a house with a new roof.

The water heater is new, the plumbing is new, the furnace is new. You are getting a house that essentially does not, and will not, need repairs for some time. I have yet to sell an existing house that did not have problems needing immediate attention. At this time in your lives, I do not feel either one of you has the time necessary to spend fiddling with your house. Your life-style and the demands in raising your family and job dictate that you should buy a house that is relatively maintenance and trouble free. You can obtain those goals only by buying a newer home.

"There are other benefits. This is the opportunity to get this house exactly the way you want it. You can put it on the lot you desire, facing the direction you desire. You can pick out the exact floor plan you want, the styles, the features, the colors of the roof, exterior, carpeting, tile, formica, vinyl. All of these opportunities allow you to tailor this house exactly the way you want it, something you simply can't do when buying an existing house."

When people are buying a new home, they are buying dreams, and you need to sell the benefits of those dreams. You can use the following: "Mike, I want you to consider something else. When you buy an existing home, you are stuck with what is there. Not only a house that is going to need immediate attention in a number of areas, but also the former owners' ideas of decorating. You are stuck with their choices of carpet color, paint schemes and decorating. You can personalize a new house to your own tastes."

"You have us sold on the price of this house and it being worth the money, but there are no drapes. Just the drapes for this house are going to cost us hundreds and maybe thousands of dollars."

"Mike and Lori, I have always considered the fact there are no drapes a real opportunity. An opportunity to decorate and customize this home so it matches your furniture, your art work, your wall hangings and your life-style."

"Well, there is still another cost you have not talked about, Jim, and that is landscaping. There is essentially no landscaping here."

"Let me ask you. Are the two of you landscaping buffs? Do you like gardening? Do you like hedges and trees? If so, I do not think you would want someone else to design and decide what your yard should look like. What you have here is a blank slate. You can create the yard exactly as you want it. You can customize the landscaping to your taste, just as you customized the color scheme, the style and so forth. I understand there is some cost, but we can build that into the price of the house. You can design the landscaping. It can be added to the loan, and you can get this house landscaped the way you want it at a cost of only a few dollars extra a month."

Specific Objections and Solutions when Working with Buyers

"This is just too big of a jump in payments from what we are currently paying."

"Your present payment is $840, and the payment on your new house is going to be $1,200. This is a difference of $360 and, yes, that is a pretty big jump. I would like you to consider the following: First, $360 can be broken down to $12 a day. If you factor in the tax benefits, there is only about an $8.50 per day difference between your present and new payment. Part of this $8.50 is going to be made up in commuting costs. Since you are closer to work, you are going to be able to save money on gas and wear and tear on your car. You will also be able to make up some of this in the form of lower utility bills, as this is a newer house with tighter insulation and a more efficient heating and cooling system. When you take all of these factors into consideration, I think you will agree that it is not quite as big a jump as it looks on the surface."

"If we do buy this house, we want the sellers to leave the range, refrigerator, freezer and washer and dryer."

"Those items are not included on the listing and were not factored into the price when the sellers put the house on the market. Although everything is negotiable, it hurts your negotiating position when it comes to the major points of the contract if you insist on asking for a number of small concessions. You have indicated you want to offer less than the listing price. If you still insist on doing that, I would suggest you not ask for these other items, to increase your chances of getting your contract accepted as is."

11

Additional Buyer Situations

THE TEST-DRIVE CLOSE

The first thing a car salesperson does when trying to sell a car is to get the prospect into the car for a test-drive. When you have your buyers in what you sense is the "right house," the time is right to get the buyers to "test-drive" the house. This brings the buyers to a frame of mind where they are mentally moving in and deciding who will get which bedroom and where the furniture will go.

After the initial tour of the house, your prospects will be ready to get back in the car and head for the next house, since that is what you have done in every other case. Naturally, you want to keep them in the house because the best place to write up a sale is on the dining-room table of the property they are considering. Upon completion of the initial showing, say something like the following: "Truman and Beth, I sense you like this house better than anything else we have seen. In fact, I would bet pretty good money you are not going to cross this off the possibility list, are you?" If you have read them right, they will say, "No, we are not crossing this off our possibility list."

Proceed by saying, "Since you are strongly considering this property, I would like the two of you to go through the entire property again. Just the two of you. I am going to sit down in the living room and read a magazine. Go over the house from top to bottom. I suggest you do this for two reasons. First of all, I want you to learn everything there is to know about this house before you consider making an offer. Second, this will help you remember what is specifically in this house. After seeing a number of properties, buyers can get confused as to what was in which house, what type of wallpaper was in the three-quarter bath, what the pattern was on the vinyl flooring in the kitchen and so forth. So for these two reasons, I would like you to reinspect the entire house, and I will be here to answer any questions you have."

If this is the correct house, one or the other, or both, will sell the house to each other. Spending this time together will help them get used to the thought of moving into the house, having it as their own, decorating it and making it theirs. When they have finished going through the house for the second time, they again are ready to get into the car. This is not what you are going to do. Only bad things can happen if they get into the car at this time. They will see a sign on another house similar to this one and say, "We haven't seen that one yet." When this happens, all the work you have accomplished will be down the drain. You will be back to square one. Even if they do want to write an offer once reaching the office, they will have trouble remembering certain aspects about the house. With this uncertainty in mind, it will be difficult for you to get them "down on paper." I suggest dialogue something like the following: "Truman and Beth, while you were going through the house, I had the chance to throw a few figures together. I would like to sit down with you and go over them. This will give you a good idea how closely this house fits into the original down payment and monthly investment you wanted to make." Proceed to The Tabletop Close.

THE TABLETOP CLOSE

"The Tabletop Close" is considered to be a natural extension of "The Test-Drive Close."

Sit down with the buyers at the kitchen or dining-room table. Have your buyers' estimated net sheets out, all financing information pertinent to their situation worked out and, of course, have a purchase agreement in plain view. Go over every entry on your buyers' estimated net sheet. As you go through the net sheet, ask questions where the answers will logically go on the purchase agreement. Try something like this.

"Beth and Truman, we originally discussed ten percent as an earnest deposit. You have indicated you want to make less than a full-price offer. To maximize your chances of getting this less-than-full-price offer accepted, I would like to suggest making a substantial earnest deposit of at least ten percent of the price. Would you be comfortable with $12,000 as an earnest deposit?"

If they say yes, they will be comfortable with that, take the purchase agreement and fill in $12,000 in the appropriate spot. When reaching the interest proration on the estimate sheet, explain that this figure will depend on what time of the month they close. This gives you an excellent opportunity to talk about closing and possession dates. When you get commitments on that, once again insert it into the purchase agreement. ("The Tabletop Close" is one variation of "The Write-Them-Up Close.")

By continually asking open-ended questions, receiving commitments and filling out the purchase agreement as you receive answers, you can smoothly move ahead for a signature.

MR. SMITH-FELT-THE-SAME-WAY CLOSE

This is frequently referred to as the *feel, felt, found close.* When your buyer expresses some interest in the house but objects to the distance from where she works, you can use this approach.

"Kathleen, I understand how you feel. This is somewhat of a longer drive from where you are currently living to your job. I happen to have sold another house in this subdivision to Kevin Schwartz. Kevin felt the same way you do, as he also works downtown. We found out that if you take Chandler Road to 13th and go north on 13th, you can arrive in downtown Omaha in approximately 15 minutes. You are now about ten minutes away from work, aren't you, Kathleen? What we are talking about here is another five minutes each way each day."

One, I understand how you *feel*. Two, someone else *felt* the same way. Three, this is the solution they came up with, and this is what they *found*. Properly introduced, the *feel*, *felt*, *found* close is one of the most potent, final closes available.

NOW-IS-THE-TIME CLOSE

This works exceptionally well with first-time buyers who are reluctant to make a decision. You have done a good job of qualifying for their wants, needs and abilities, have lead them through the entire home-buying process and have found the right house. They are nervous and are having a tough time making a decision. It is now time for you to play the father or mother figure, and age has nothing to do with this.

"Fred and Cindy, you told me that if we found the house that truly met your wants and needs, you were ready to buy. We have spent enough time looking at properties to know that this house fits the bill. Now is the time to buy. If you hesitate, you run the risk of losing it to another buyer. That is a strong possibility when you consider how nice this place is, the great condition it is in and the very attractive financing being offered."

THE REDUCTION CLOSE

"The Reduction Close" is used to take a seemingly insurmountable objection and reduce it to smaller parts to be acceptable to the prospect.

An effective reduction close is reducing dollars per day. Say the payment on a house the prospects like is $90 a month more than they feel comfortable with. Ninety dollars a month breaks down to $3 a day. Depending on the buyers' tax bracket, it may be only $2.25. "Is $2.25 a day a good reason to not live in the house you want?"

Another effective reduction technique is reducing distance to time. Your prospects may object that the property is too far from where they work. Ask them what part of town they would feel more comfortable with in relation to their jobs and convert the distance between the two into time. "Yes, that is three miles closer to your job. However, this property is only five minutes farther from where you work because of the interstate highway. Five minutes' extra traveling time per day going each direction is not a reason to not buy a house, is it, Mr. Smith?"

You can counter size objections by converting them to how those rooms are used. Perhaps the buyers will object that the bedrooms are too small. In actuality, people spend little waking time in their bedrooms. You can counter this objection with the following:

"Bud and Marny, I understand the bedrooms may be smaller than you like. The builder felt it would be better to put a proportionally larger amount of the square footage in the areas where you will spend most of your time, the family room, living room and kitchen. You have expressed a maximum amount you want to spend in purchasing a house, and I am sure your intention is to buy a house that has the most usable square footage for the money. I think you will agree that square footage in the living room, dining room and kitchen are far more usable than having slightly bigger bedrooms."

THE WILL-THEY-TAKE-LESS CLOSE

This not only entails intelligent salesmanship, but also tact and caution to avoid violating most states' license laws. Most states prohibit quoting anything other than the listed price and terms. Any implication that the sellers will take less is a legal and ethical violation to be avoided. Fortunately, there is a closing technique that will allow you to get the buyers to write an offer without violating your fiduciary responsibilities to your sellers. It goes something like this. Buying prospect: "Will the sellers take $88,000?" Salesperson: "Patrick, not only do *I* not know what the sellers will accept, in many instances, the sellers themselves do not know what they will take until they actually see an offer. Although the property is priced at $89,000, I would be willing to submit an offer of $88,000, to see how the sellers react. Are you prepared to make an offer for $88,000 at this time?" You never want to pass up the chance to write an offer. When you have an offer, you at least have something to work with. Try to write the best offer you can, but do not imply what your sellers will do when you cannot know for sure.

I have had sellers say, "I am not selling for less than $76,000. If it is less than $76,000, do not even bring it over. I am going to hold firm to $76,000, or I will keep it forever." The next week I would receive an offer for $73,000, present it and, without a word, the sellers who just a week ago said, "We are not taking less than $76,000," will accept the offer as is. I do not know if the sellers are willing to take less, but I am certainly willing to write an offer in an effort to find out.

CLOSING WITH INVESTOR BUYERS

Most investor buyers are looking for the steal of the century. They want to make a killing and will likely start out with a totally ridiculous offer. This is counterproductive if they are looking at a good property they would like to own. As we discussed earlier, starting out with a crazy, lowball offer frequently destroys the investors' negotiating position and actually decreases their chances of purchasing the property at any kind of reasonable price. In addition to the previously discussed techniques that can be used with all buyers, the following two approaches work very well when working with investors.

The market data approach.   Compile and prepare the same market data material you use when trying to list a property. It will include solds, pendings, expireds and on the markets that are comparable to the property the investors are considering. Naturally, the buyers will want to get a better deal than what most of the comparables are selling for, but this will at least get them to make a reasonable offer, increasing the chances of making the transaction work.

Work an Internal Rate of Return.   Although many investment buyers are just as hopelessly impulse-oriented as most homebuyers, some will listen to reason. In these cases, it is an effective technique for you to calculate an Internal Rate of Return (IRR) or a Financial Management Rate of Return (FMRR) and show the investors what their yield will be for one, three, five and ten years, using conservative projections for increases in expenses and rent.

At times, the investment buyers' main concern will be initial negative cash flow. The answer again is to prepare, present and explain the Internal Rate of Return, based on cash flow after taxes. Many times a negative cash flow will be a breakeven or sometimes even a positive cash flow when the tax considerations are put into effect. Under the Tax Reform Act of 1986, this varies greatly with the buyers' income and the number of investment properties they own. If the investors' are planning on holding the property long-term, at least five to seven years, the negative cash flow will commonly only project out for the first year or two, and should not in itself be a reason not to purcahse the property.

Another legitimate concern of investment buyers is being able to resell the property once it is purchased. The best solution to this is to sell your investors well-located, well-built properties. Harry Helmsley, one of the most successful real estate investors of all time, has a rule he never violates: Invest only in well-located properties. Historically, well-located properties increase in value far more quickly than poorly located properties. Buyers pay a premium for a well-located property for a very good reason. They are paying a premium because of the potential. The potential for well-located, well-designed and properly constructed properties is far greater than buying physically or locationally distressed properties. Well-located properties also draw the best tenants, a distinct advantage.

Another way to alleviate the fear of resale problems when selling less expensive investment properties is to sell the buyers on obtaining assumable financing. The VA offers financing for owner-occupied one to four units, and the FHA offers a viable investment loan with less than 20 percent down. Both of these loans are assumable to a subsequent buyer with certain conditions. A variation of this is to buy properties that already have assumable FHA or VA financing. Even if the property values escalate greatly, there is the chance of a subsequent buyer getting a wraparound mortgage, a second mortgage or, in some instances, the seller can consider a seller-carry-back vehicle.

Many first-time investment buyers are concerned with property management problems. They do not understand how to screen tenants, how to set up a firm and consistent collection policy or how to work with tenants when rent payments are late. There are two solutions: the first is to give them a basic education on steps they can take to ensure they are adequately screening their tenants. Caveat: Explain to them the restraints property managers are under when it comes to Federal Fair Housing and local Fair Housing laws. Make sure they fully understand these when you are giving them any advice on how to screen tenants or manage their property. If your state has adopted the Uniform Residential Landlord and Tenant Act, it is good to give your investment buyers a copy of this act, as it tells them what they can and cannot do when dealing with tenants.

Another solution for fear of management problems is to refer your investment buyers to a good property manager. Depending on the size of the cash flow, this may not be feasible in the first few years of the investment. But if it is, this will alleviate the investors' fears and make investing in real estate much easier than they thought it could be.

12

Negotiating with Sellers

PRESENTING GOOD OFFERS

It is the moral and ethical duty of every real estate salesperson to get "good contracts" accepted as is. This is because the risks in countering an already good offer far outweigh the potential gains. The following is a systematic, persistent approach to getting the sellers to see the logic in accepting the offer as is.

Working Small to Big in Obtaining Conditional Agreements

The idea here is to clear up all small or minor points before ever approaching the major points of discussion. Let's take an example: You have a property listed for $83,000. The range oven and refrigerator are excluded on the listing. You have received a purchase agreement for $80,000 in which the buyers request the range and the refrigerator to stay.

All the market data you have collected—final sales, pending sales, expireds and houses currently on the market—indicate that $80,000 is a very reasonable and solid offer. Looking at it objectively, it is easy to say that a range and refrigerator are not and reason not to sell a house. However, many sales are lost on minor items of this nature. We have to understand how a buyer's complex emotions work to keep the small items small and keep the sellers' eyes focused on the entire overall picture. The way we do this is to verbally obtain a conditional agreement on all minor items before showing the sellers the actual purchase agreement or discussing any major points of negotiation. The major points of negotiation are most often price, discount points to be paid by the sellers or concessions regarding early possession by the buyers.

In the above described case, you should obtain a concession on the range and refrigerator before actually taking the contract out of your briefcase. You can do it like this:

"Dan and Susan, this is a very good contract. However, there are a few points that differ from the way we originally listed the property. As I am sure you remember, when we listed the property, we excluded the range and refrigerator, so you could take them to your new house. The buyers have requested that you leave the range and refrigerator and include it in the sales price of the house. Let me ask you one question. If we can produce a high enough net, and if the other terms and the possession are agreeable to you, would you leave the range and the refrigerator?"

In almost every case they are going to say, "Yes, we would leave the range and refrigerator if we got enough money and everything else is acceptable." As you look in their eyes, you can see them thinking, "How much? How much? Tell us about the contract." This is perfectly acceptable. Present the rest of the contract. When you get to the price and say it is $80,000, they reply, "We were hoping to do a little bit better; that is a little less than we said we would take." They are mildly disappointed. If this happens, you are in relatively good shape. After presenting the contract and going through the following closes, they will ordinarily accept it. Small to big is the optimal approach.

Let's take a look at what happens if you introduce the major points of the negotiation first. Say you take out the purchase agreement, they look at the price, and they say, "Oh, $80,000 is less than we wanted. We hoped to do better." Again, using a series of closes, they recognize and accept the fact that $80,000 is a very good offer, and they are ready to accept it. At that point, you say, "Oh, yes, by the way, the buyers want you to leave the range and the refrigerator." The following reaction is frequently swift and very strong: "We just gave them $3,000, and now they want us to throw in the range and the refrigerator!"

Let's analyze this. The agent who used the second approach got exactly what he deserved. It is the nature of negotiation that any minor items introduced after the major points of negotiation becomes a major item in itself, no matter how small it is. In most cases, the sellers are emotionally drained after you finish discussing the major point, in this case, the price. Anything introduced after this will create a major stumbling block.

Introducing the minor points first and getting conditional agreements keeps the minor points minor. Save the major points of negotiation for last.

Explain the Complete Purchase Agreement and Net Sheet

When making a major decision, many people use the following defense mechanism: They focus on one small portion or one small factor of the decision and do not look at the overall consequences of the entire agreement. Sellers will often spend more time arguing over the family-room drapes than they will over $1,000 or $2,000 in price. We do the job we were hired for by getting our sellers to look at the entire purchase agreement in a logical manner.

One of the best ways of doing this is to explain the entire purchase agreement and net sheet before allowing any discussion. Introduce it as follows:

> "Patrick and Kori, I have found that it is best for the sellers of a property if they allow me to explain the entire purchase agreement

and net sheet before we discuss any individual items. It is important to see the overall picture before you can intelligently discuss
any one part of the contract. With your permission, I would like
to do this."

It is relatively easy to get the sellers to agree to this. By doing
this, you keep the discussion focused on the major points. This
helps the sellers focus on the forest, not the individual trees. If the
sellers wait until you explain the entire contract, they are going to
be ready to hop right in as soon as you are through with your explanation. When they hop right in, they will have completely forgotten the minor points that were not really a reason not to sell
their house, and they will focus on the major points: price, closing date, possession, personal property items and terms. This approach keeps the sellers from using up their patience and
attention span on minor points.

Obtaining the Acceptance

Your approach in obtaining acceptance of the agreement will depend upon the sellers' reaction when you complete your explanations. Completely explain the purchase agreement and net sheet
and then ask, "Mark and Kathy, do you have any questions regarding the price, how the net was calculated, projected closing
and possession dates and any of the contingencies?" If they say,
"No, we don't have any questions," you should first try the silent
assumptive close.

Turn over the purchase agreement, put the carbon in it, fill in
the acceptance, sign it where needed, put two x's down, turn it
around, put the pen down and be completely silent and still.

Give the sellers an opportunity to accept the purchase agreement. Sellers cannot and will not sign an agreement if you are talking. If you are talking, you are not giving the sellers the space, the
time and, most importantly, the opportunity they need to affix
their autographs.

They may sign it at this point and they may not. If they do
not, proceed with the following closing sequence. Throughout
your entire presentation, stop periodically, be silent and give
them ample opportunities to sign the offer.

The sellers have two choices: they can sign either the agreement or come up with an objection. Either way, you have taken a meaningful step forward. If they sign the agreement, the job is done. If they come up with an objection, you now know what you need to work on.

If there is a negative reaction or objection, go through the following series of closes. One basic technique I use throughout all of these closes is the following: Every time they come up with an objection, say, "Before you make a final decision, I would like you to consider one more thing." Always assume they have not reached a final decision until they make the decision that is right for their situation. Try the following three-options close.

The three-options close. If they are not ready to accept the contract, you can use what I call "The Three-Options Close."

"Tim and Tamara, before you make a decision, I would like to explain the three options all sellers have when a contract is presented to them. The first option is to accept it exactly the way it is written. As soon as it is accepted, we have a valid, binding contract. We will contact the buyers and inform them that it has been accepted, so we have mutual assent, sometimes referred to as a meeting of the minds. We will then deposit the earnest deposit check into our trust account, and we've got a pending sale. That is option one: Accept it as it is.

"Option two is to reject the contract. For all practical purposes, this ends negotiations unless the buyers want to resubmit an entirely new offer. In most cases, this is inadvisable unless there is a totally unacceptable aspect of the purchase agreement or the purchasers, such as bad credit and unacceptable seller-assisted financing, among others.

"The third option all sellers have with every contract is to propose a counteroffer. At this point, pause. If you look closely at their eyes, you will see them thinking, 'Counteroffer— counteroffer—counteroffer.' After the pause, say the following: 'Tim and Tamara, *sellers should never counter an offer unless it is a point they are willing to lose the sale over,* as any counteroffer automatically voids the original offer.' Let me give you an example. The sellers receive an offer, and it is acceptable in all respects, except the buyers want to close and have possession on July 17, a day earlier than the sellers would have liked. The sellers say, 'Let's counter and give them possession July 18.' They proceed to make the counteroffer in writing. Unfortunately, the buyers are suffering from 'buyers' remorse,' and they turn the counteroffer down. The sellers' first response is to say, 'Okay, we will accept the original offer.' The sellers cannot do that because any counteroffer voids the original offer.

"I would like you to carefully consider the consequences of making a counteroffer. Unless it is something significant and a reason over which you are willing to lose the buyers, I would refrain from making any counter whatsoever. Tim and Tamara, if I were you, I would accept this agreement the way it is." If they are ready to accept it, great. If not, move on to the next close.

The buyer-psychology close   "I understand how you feel, Frank and Betty. Before we make a decision here, I would like you to fully understand the entire contract and how everything works. Let's talk about buyer psychology for a minute. Buyer psychology is a very delicate thing. We are sitting here considering this offer. It is a big and difficult decision for you. I understand how you feel, but I want you to try to put yourself in the buyers' shoes for just a few moments. Consider what the buyers are going through this very minute. They are sitting on pins and needles in their apartment, waiting for this offer to be accepted or rejected. They are undoubtedly in a highly nervous state. Let me tell you how buyer psychology works and how human nature plays tricks on buyers in this situation. Say you accept this offer exactly as is. We call the buyers and say, 'Congratulations, Bob and Sue. You have just bought a house.' Ordinarily, the first thing the buyers do is justify their purchase. They start saying, 'We looked at a lot of houses. The loan officer did say we were qualified. It is in the right school district. It is the floor plan we wanted, and it looks like the best house we could get for the money.' Buyers customarily justify their actions when their contract is accepted."

Let's look at what their typical reaction would be if the contract is not accepted. The buyers are called and the real estate agent says, 'Pretty good news. They did not accept it as is, but they only made some minor changes in a counteroffer.' Almost immediately, the buyers start having regrets, frequently saying, 'We really haven't looked at many houses. We made this decision in a pretty quick manner.' Some buyers think this is a signal that fate has told them they should not buy this house. In almost every case, they start having second thoughts.

"Buyer psychology is a very delicate thing. It is quite easy to chase a buyer away. One of the things that triggers a buyer's urge to run away is a counteroffer. We want to avoid the buyer experiencing these regrets and second-thought emotions. If you decide to counter, I want you to make sure it is for a reason that makes this contract, without question, unacceptable the way it is written."

The risk/gain factor.   If your buyers still want to counter on a minor item, you can use the following approach: "I understand your desire to make a counteroffer, as this is not exactly what you wanted. Let's consider what we have to gain if we counter this one small item versus what is at risk." Another way we could say it is, "What do we have to lose by countering this if the counteroffer scares the buyers away? We are losing the entire sale of the house. The risk you are considering is far greater than the potential gain."

The market-data close.   "Dan and Susan, I want you to make this decision based on fact and not emotion. I want to take the time necessary to explain every aspect of this contract and how it relates to your house. Let's review the market data we looked at when we placed the house on the market, plus recent final sales, pendings, new listings on the market and so forth."

Proceed to review the market data and take enough time to thoroughly compare their house and this contract to every final sale. If this is a good contract, these final sales are going to bolster the convictions of the sellers that they probably cannot do better. Do the same with every pending sale on which you have obtained information. Proceed by comparing this contract and their house with every expired listing. Show them facts and figures that prove the contract is "good." Tell them how they could end up in the "graveyard of expired listings." Next, review the new competition, everything for sale in that area and in that price range. "Dan and Susan, more houses are being put on the market all of the time. They are your new competition. You are competing with every one of these houses for the comparatively few buyers active in the marketplace. We have a buyer who wants to buy your house over all of the others. A buyer who is ready to pay you a fair price. I know what you are thinking. 'How can he say it is a fair price? What makes him the guy who determines if this is a fair price?' Dan and Susan, I have not determined if it is a fair price. The marketplace determines what the fair range of value is, and that is why we are looking at this data. This data, not me, says that this is a very good offer." Keep yourself under control, and be quiet. Give them the opportunity to sign the contract. If they are still not ready to make that final decision, move on as follows.

The marketplace-feedback close. I sometimes think of this close as "The 106-Reasons-Why-Nobody-Wants-to-Buy-Your-House Close." This consists of sharing all the marketplace feedback we discussed earlier in the text. Open-house feedback, tour feedback, thanks-for-showing-my-listing feedback and so forth. Naturally, your sellers do not want to see this material again, and I do not blame them. It is a reminder that people are not interested in their house, and, at times, this is taken as harsh criticism. This is difficult for them to accept because some homeowners have strong emotional attachments to their house. We must change their way of thinking. Until we can get them to see their house through the eyes of the buyer, we are sunk. At this point, if they are still hesitant to accept the contract, it is time to find out why.

The boil-down close. The boil-down close consists of discovering the true points of contention. We have to get down to specifics. Try dialogue something like this: "Mike and Lori, I sense you are not comfortable with this contract. There must be a specific problem with this contract that is keeping you from accepting it. I would like to know why this contract is unacceptable to you, so we can work on resolving the problem." We are trying to bring their fears, concerns and objections into perspective. If they are vague in their reasons and excuses, you must press on and find out why.

If they eventually decide to refuse the contract, which hopefully will not happen, we must determine the best counteroffer they are willing to make. Phrases many salespeople find helpful at this point are as follows: 'Ten years from now, will it make any real difference in your life if you make a concession on this one point? I don't think it will.' 'Ten years from now, will it make a real difference to you if you do not put this sale together and end up staying in this house for another four months? Yes, I do think that's something that will be remembered and regretted ten years from now. I would hate to see this happen to you."

Another variation of this is, "Joe and Carol, we have been working on the sale of this house for more than three months. This is the first serious offer we have had, and I think it is time to bite the bullet on the small stuff and get this house sold and closed."

The buy-it-back close.   This can profitably be used whenever the sellers want to counter the price. Let's say the sellers want to counter the price by $1,000. Any objective person who is not involved in this agreement knows that $1,000 is not a reason not to sell the house. Any reasonable person would say that if the sale is within $1,000 of what the sellers want, it is foolish not to take it. We need to remember that the sellers are operating on high-octane emotion and not logic. We need them to see the logic of that position. Use dialogue such as the following when your sellers say they want to counter for $1,000.

> "Ron and Patty, I want you to consider the fact that the house is sold. All you have to do is sign the contract. I will call the buyers and inform them it is accepted, and we have a binding contract. We put the earnest deposit into the bank, and it is sold. You want to counter this for $81,000. If the buyers turn down your counter and walk, in effect, you have bought your house back after it has been sold for $80,000. You have bought it back for $81,000. I do not think you want to do this. I want you to consider a few other things about this $1,000. An extra $1,000 in price is not $1,000 in

net. In this sale you are being asked to pay discount points. When you take into consideration the sales commission, the discount points and documentary stamps you are not going to get an extra thousand. It is going to be more like $880. So, in effect, you did not buy it back for $1,000. You bought it back for $880.

The four-months-carrying-charges close. "Rick and Diane, we have been on the market now for four months. It took us that long to get a decent offer. If we lose this offer over $1,000, or in actuality $880, we may not see another offer for another four months. Let's estimate what four months' principal, interest, taxes and insurance amount to. We can also throw in maintenance and, if you move, double payments. If we wait four months for the second buyer as we did for the first, you can end up losing far, far more than this $880 you want to counter over."

Another variation of this is the *Double-Payments Close*. "Dan and Kathy, Dan is supposed to report to his new job in Salt Lake City in five weeks. If we do not put this sale together now, you are going to end up with two payments. Either a house payment here and a rent payment on an apartment in Salt Lake City if Dan moves out by himself or, if you both go, you will probably have two house payments. Most people feel a tremendous amount of pressure when they are making two payments. Commonly they will say, 'We can make two payments for a couple of months if that is what it is going to take to get the money I want out of this house.' But once those double payments start coming due, the pressure increases and the regrets set in. With the price of real estate in Salt Lake City and knowing what type of house you want, one extra month can wipe out this supposed gain you are trying to obtain."

The there-is-no-guarantee close. "Dan and Susan, I understand you want to do better than $80,000. I would love to sell this house for more than $80,000 because the more we sell this house for, the more I get paid. But you are trying to sell your house at the sellers' price, your price. I can't sell this house at your price. I can only sell it for what it is worth, what a buyer will pay us. Right now we have a valid buyer who is willing to pay $80,000. You are going to try to squeeze this buyer for more. If this buyer walks, you are assuming there is another current and potential buyer willing to pay you $81,000. That is not always true." This close will easily segue into:

The first-offer-is-often-the-best close. "Eric and Bridget, for a number of reasons, the first offer received on a parcel of real estate is frequently the best, and there is a good reason for this. For every parcel of real estate there is one best buyer. One buyer who is most qualified to buy this house. One buyer who has the highest interest level in this house. One buyer whose needs, wants and abilities most perfectly match this house. This is the buyer who is going to pay you the highest price for this house.

"Logic tells us that the first person to make an offer on a house is most often this one best buyer. If you chase away the best buyer through unrealistic expectations and unwise counteroffers, you will have to wait around for the second best buyer. The second best buyer is not always as willing to pay what that first best buyer was willing to pay. In fact, many times the second best buyer will fail to come up to the original offer made by your first buyer. The landscape of unsold houses is filled with instances where sellers received a good offer in the first two weeks on the market, but lost the buyers by making a counteroffer. They thought their house was so desirable they would be able to get 'their price.' Time would go by and three, six and sometimes eight and ten months later, they are in a position where they would jump at the initial offer. I do not want to see you put yourself in that situation."

The buyers-are-at-the-max close. "Carl and Lavonne, you are only looking at this offer from your own point of view. It is human nature to do that. I want you to think about the buyers for a moment. We have prequalified the buyers. In fact, the buyers have already seen a loan officer at First Guarantee Mortgage. According to the officer and according to our qualification figures, these buyers are at the maximum loan for which they can most likely qualify. The buyers are somewhat apprehensive, and I can imagine how they must feel right now. They do not have to buy this house. If we make it difficult for them by asking more than they can afford to pay, there is no real loss to them. I understand that you do not have to sell this house, but it is going to create a far more immediate and critical problem for you if you don't. You have got more to lose than the buyers."

The reversal technique.   "John and Sarah, in front of us is the market data relevant to your house: solds, pendings, expireds, on the markets, amount of average negotiation and average sales time on the market. Computers have enabled us to compile and evaluate enormous amounts of information quite easily. This market data is available to agents, sellers and buyers. In today's marketplace, many buyers now ask the real estate salesperson they are working with to do market research and show them what properties have been selling for in an area. In addition, these buyers have been researching the marketplace themselves by looking at houses, comparing neighborhoods, financing programs, school districts and other market data. They may even have a better idea of what this house is worth than you.

"I am going to ask you a very blunt question, and I want you to answer me truthfully. If we reversed the situation and you were the buyers with this same market data in front of you, would you pay more than $80,000 for this house?" Pause. "I don't think you would, and I don't think the buyers will either."

The review-the-motivations close.   "Let's get out a sheet of paper and list all of the original motivations you shared with me when I first listed this house. Number one, you wanted to net enough money out of the sale of this house to close on the house you are buying in Phoenix. Two, you wanted to avoid double payments. Three, you wanted to avoid renting an apartment and having your family split up between two cities for months on end. Four, you wanted to obtain a fair price for this house. Five, you wanted a timely sale, a timely sale being one that would allow you to do all of the above. This contract fulfills all of your original motivations. In plain words, this contract will complete all of your requirements. Let's fulfill all of these original motivations you had. Let's sign this contract and get the wheels in motion."

The if-I-were-you close. If your sellers have all the facts and they are still struggling with making a decision, you can use the following approach: "Beth and John, it is a big decision, and I understand it is a big decision. It is a decision people make relatively few times in their lives. I understand how many sellers, and possibly you, feel. You do not buy and sell houses every day, and you have been given a lot of information that sometimes seems overwhelming and confusing. Because of these and other factors, sellers commonly feel they are ill-equipped to make a knowledgeable decision. I empathize with you. I can understand how difficult this is and how big of a decision it is.

"I negotiate sales every day for a living and have handled literally hundreds of home sales. Perhaps my perspective will help you decide what to do. If our roles were reversed, and I knew what I know about real estate, I would accept this offer right now. I consider it a good offer and one you are unlikely to better. I think this offer should be accepted as is, and I would not tell you that if I did not truly believe it."

We-need-to-get-an-appraisal. "I understand your motivations in wanting to get another $1,000 for the house. Our market data tells us that $80,000 is on the very high end of what an appraiser can justify for a loan appraisal on this house. Yes, even if we do get $81,000, we still have to get an appraisal. All of the final sales we have collected imply we are unlikely to get an appraisal for $81,000. We will probably be lucky to get an appraisal for $80,000. We are again putting ourselves in a risky position with a chance of absolutely no gain, even if the proposed counteroffer of $1,000 is accepted."

The Ben Franklin close. "To help you make the best decision possible, I am going to suggest you do what Ben Franklin did whenever he had a big decision. Ben would draw a line down the middle of a blank piece of paper. [Get out a piece of paper and start filling it in.] On one side he would list the benefits of making one decision. On the other side of the line he would list the benefits if he made the decision the other way.

"On the left side, let's list the benefits of accepting this as is. Number one, the pressure is off. The house is finally sold. I know you have been concerned and somewhat about this house not selling. Number two, you have the peace of mind knowing that significant progress is being made to close a pending transaction on this house. Three, it will give you the money you need to close on the house you want to buy. Four, your kids will not have to change schools in the middle of a semester. Five, it will avoid your making double payments." Continue writing down every possible good reason for them to accept the contract. "In the right-hand column, let's write down all the positive things that can happen if you decide to make a counteroffer. I can only think of one. You *might* get another $880."

We-need-time-to-think-about-this close. "You are feeling an enormous amount of pressure at this time, aren't you? I understand completely. That is an entirely natural feeling. It is impossible to make a decision of this size without feeling some pressure.

"When people feel pressured, the first thing that comes to mind is they need more time to consider the decision. I understand that. Tonight, I have given you all of the practical ramifications of this contract. I have told you what you would net and have given you the pros and cons of countering or accepting the contract. I have also discussed every aspect of this transaction that should enter your decision making, and I still sense you are not ready to make a decision. Most likely, you would like to discuss it between the two of you without my being here. Am I right?" In almost every case you are going to get an affirmative answer. In fact, they think, "Oh, good, he's going to leave. The pressure is gone. We don't have to do anything with this right now." But we cannot allow that to happen. Most purchase agreements have immediate acceptance deadlines. In effect, not accepting by the stated deadline is the same as rejecting the offer. Try dialogue something like this: "I understand why you feel that way, and I want to accommodate you. Unfortunately, we have a deadline on this contract, and we do not have the luxury of having a day or two to decide. We need to come up with an answer now, or for all practical purposes, we are telling the buyer we are

not going to sell. To make this easier for you, I am going to suggest the following: I am going to go into the family room, turn on
the Cubs game and give you all of the time you need. This will
give you time to discuss it between the two of you, without me in
the room, while allowing me to answer any questions you may
have." Stand up, go into the family room, shut the door, turn on
the television and relax. At this point, the acceptance is probably
already in the bag. These people just need time to justify taking
the contract to each other and themselves. In fact, if one is clearly
the decision maker and want's to take the contract, you are going
to be relaxing while he or she does your job for you. Who is in a
better position to convince the doubting Thomas that this contract should be accepted than the spouse? If it is not accepted by
the time you have used this close, you have done all you can do,
and it is time to let somebody else have a crack at it.

13

Additional Seller Situations

Let's take a situation where the buyers make a $70,000 offer on a property listed at $80,000. The fair market value is approximately $75,000.

We approach our sellers and present the contract. Naturally, the sellers are insulted because in their eyes the offer is ridiculously low. Of course it is not any more ridiculously low than the asking price of the property was high. Your sellers want to counter at the full price, or in this example, let's say they want to go down a thousand and counter at $79,000. If this happens, you are on the road to ruin. Let's say the sellers counter at $79,000. If we can get the buyers to make another counter, we might get them up to $71,000. We go back to our sellers and our sellers say, "Well if the buyers are going to be that way, we will only go down to $78,000." You go back to the buyers. Maybe they will come up to $72,000. This is where we run into trouble. *In negotiations, it is not so much the size of concessions as it is the number of concessions.*

The more times you go back and forth, the more pride starts entering into the mix. The sellers' position is, "I have gone down twice, and I will be darned if I am going to reduce my asking price a third time." Meanwhile, the buyers are blurting, "We have raised our initial offer twice! This guy wants blood."

The fact that neither one of them is anywhere near a reasonable price for the property does not enter into their thinking. Back-and-forth wrangling destroys sales. The more we go back and forth making small concessions, the more likely the buyers are to walk. By doing this, the sellers are making it difficult for the buyers to buy their house. The more difficult the sellers make it for the buyers, the more likely the sellers are to own that house for a long, long time. The following is a good remedy for this situation:

"Rob and Ashley, I understand your desire to counter at or near the full price. However, this complicates negotiations and lessens our chances of making this work. I am going to be frank with you. We all know this house is not worth $80,000. The market data and marketplace feedback we have collected tells us that trying to get $80,000 or $79,000 out of the house is unrealistic. We also know from the same market data that the house is worth more than $70,000. This offer is less than I would recommend you to accept."

"The reason we received an offer for $70,000 is because we are overpriced. I would like to ask you one question, Rob and Ashley. If you could get an offer from these buyers for $75,000, and you knew that was as good an offer you could get from those buyers, would you accept that offer today? Think about it for just a moment if you would like. Again, assume the most you could sell it for today was $75,000. Would you take it? My advice to you would be to seriously consider taking an offer at that price. Would you? If you would, I suggest you counter at $75,000 right now."

Rob and Ashley will probably reply'. "But if we do that, they are just going to make another counter of $72,500 and then what?" "Then we go back at $75,000 again. We don't have to take any counteroffer they make. Rob and Ashley, I would like to give you one of the basic guidelines we follow in negotiations. *The quicker the negotiations get close to what the final sales price, terms, condition and possession should be, the more likely the pur-chase agreement will be negotiated and accepted.*

"Ashley and Rob, you will increase your chances of selling the house to these buyers if we counter at what you will take. Here is my suggestion: Counter this price at $75,000. I will meet with the selling salesperson and inform that person that this is your bottom dollar. To bolster our chances, I am going to give the selling salesperson our market data, which shows how we arrived at our price. The selling salesperson can then show this to the buyers and explain how we formulated the counter and why it is our bottom dollar."

An alternative approach is as follows: "Tony and Megan, there are many different approaches to negotiation. Let's talk about how lawyers negotiate when a case is headed to court. One lawyer starts out offering to pay nothing. The other lawyer starts out saying his client will accept one million. (This is said humorously.) The lawyers write letters, make phone calls and make no concessions for months on end. Ten minutes before the case goes to trial, they agree to $60,000.

"This is a legitimate negotiating technique. Both lawyers know that the longer they stall, the better chance the other side will make a major concession. Although valid in a 'have to settle' situation, this approach to negotiation will *not* work in real estate sales. The reason it works for the lawyers is because the two sides negotiating are forced into reaching a settlement. When people are buying a parcel of real estate, they do not have to negotiate until a settlement is reached. Buyers can walk away from the negotiations at any time. Therefore, if the sellers make the negotiations so difficult that the problems outweigh the buyers' desire to purchase the house, they have lost the buyers. Although I want you to get every cent you can out of the sale of this house, I also do not want to lose a sale that we will have trouble duplicating in the future."

Sellers do not want to carry back part of their proceeds in the form of payments.   In times of high interest rates, it is often helpful for the sellers to carry back part or all of their proceeds in the form of payments. There are a number of valid reasons for them to avoid this. First, most sellers want to get all of their money at closing. Second, they are afraid they will have a tough time collecting their money. Third, they feel there is a risk of losing the money that is carried back. To make it click, we must explain how the sellers would benefit from a carry back and what type of security they would have to have to make sure they will get their money.

"John and Christa, our original goal was to cash out at the time of closing. Unfortunately, we have not been able to do that. Here is a contract offering a fair price for the house that will allow you to close the sale in time to minimize the disruption of your move. The major stumbling block is this $5,000 the buyers are requesting that you take back in the form of payments. At this point, you need to make a difficult decision. You can take this offer and cash out, which is not particularly desirable to you, or you can turn the offer down and hope a better buyer and offer come by later.

"We have explored the possibilities. The buyer will be coming up with all of the money they have at closing. They are $5,000 short. Simply put, you can either take this $5,000 in the form of payments or not sell your house to these people. If you decide to do that, we go back on the market. We all want to avoid that."

"If you are willing to play banker for $5,000, the next logical question is, 'How do I know they will make the payments to me on time?' Every secured real estate loan must have two instruments. A promise to pay, technically called a promissory note, and a security instrument. The two most commonly used security instruments are mortgages and trust deeds. Of these two, the trust deed provides the greatest security because it allows for the quickest foreclosure in the event of a default by the buyers. [Not all states allow the use of trust deeds. If your state does not, you will have to modify this and explain the best protection available to sellers in your state.] Let me ask you a question: If you could be assured that you have the fullest protection under the law to collect these payments if the buyers default, would you consider carrying back these payments?" This will frequently quell the sellers' concerns and allow you to continue negotiations and consummate the sell.

Sellers get frustrated and stop thinking rationally. Mark Mc-Cormick, in his book *What They Don't Teach You in Harvard Business School*, contends that the first parties in the transaction who act emotionally usually hurt their position and end up with no agreement or a less favorable agreement. This requires that we keep our sellers on an even emotional keel and keep them from getting upset and revengeful. To be effective, the salespeople must stay calm when their buyers and sellers are upset, frustrated or just damn mad.

If you stay calm when your sellers blow their tops and start acting foolishly, all the chips go to your side of the table. When they do settle down, they usually feel regretful and apologetic. The best way to deal with anyone who is upset is to remain calm and rational. Continue to be very nice, even though they are treating you in the rudest of ways. This is the quickest way to bring them back to earth and ready to negotiate in a serious way.

The problem with runaway emotions is particularly difficult when working with sellers because they confuse selling their house with selling their home. They are not selling their home. Their home is where their family is. It consists of the people they love, their pets, their furnishings and their artwork. The house is just where that home is currently located. Many sellers develop an emotional attachment to their house and think it is worth more money because they have enjoyed raising their children and have gone through the joys and struggles of life in that house. This demands tact. Stress that the most important factor to them should be effecting a timely sale at a fair price. The sellers' main focus should be on the sales price, net and closing and possession dates, not on their personal opinion of the buyers.

Sometimes the personalities of the buyers can be used to advantage. If the sellers like the "looks" of the buyers, they may be likely to negotiate a sale at an even lesser price than they would in many other instances.

Sellers feel the offer is ridiculous and want to reject it rather than counter it. Most buyers want to negotiate either the listed price, terms or condition of the property offered for sale. If you have buyers who insist on "fishing" and make a ludicrous offer, write it up. You, the listing salesperson, present the offer to the sellers, and the sellers are outraged at the crazy price or terms of the offer. They want to flat out reject it. In fact, they are so insulted, they say they won't even write "rejection" across the front.

It is your job to keep the negotiations alive. "Carl and Cindy, I have to present this offer, and my manager requires proof of presentation, so if nothing else, I would like you to write "rejected" across the front. You can use a felt-tipped pen and write it in big block letters and sign it underneath the rejection if you like. But I need to show that I presented this offer. [Pause.] Even if you want to reject it, I would like you to consider an effort to save these buyers. Consider countering this offer at the full listed price and terms and give them 24 hours to accept or reject it. Many times legitimate buyers will make a ridiculous initial offer to see how the sellers will respond. These low initial offers often have the opposite effect of what was intended and your reaction is proof of that. These are legitimate buyers, and a flat-out rejection could chase them away.

"By making a full-price counteroffer with a 24-hour deadline, we will find out if these people are real buyers. There is no guarantee they will take it. There is no guarantee they will even rewrite a more reasonable offer. However, the best way to find out if we have buying prospects and not just buying suspects is to leave the door open a crack, so they can come in if they are truly interested."

One of the owners becomes upset.   When presenting the contract to a couple and one of them is highly upset, you need to let that person blow off some steam and remove the hostility that has taken place. This is best done by continuing to talk to the calm person in a way that will allow the upset person to settle down. You can use dialogue something like this: "Sheri, I understand why your husband is upset at this contract. It is not the terms or price he was looking for, but we do have potential buyers. If we will sit down and take a look at it, we can analyze it and decide what steps we want to take. If you both decide you want to reject the contract after reviewing it, I will understand your decision."

Keep your perspective. When handling difficult negotiations, your sellers may say things that could be taken personally and may offend you. Understand that these statements are not personally motivated. Sellers often regret statements of this nature at a later time. They were upset at the situation they were in and not at you when they made their comments. You happened to be the focal point.

Successful salespeople have a tremendous amount of empathy for their clients. They understand their sellers are under a great deal of stress, especially when they must make a decision when none of the choices seem favorable. Regretfully, their reaction to this high stress situation is to lash out at the person nearest to them. In most cases, it is you, the listing salesperson. When they say rude and, sometimes, insulting remarks, they are not upset with you. Stay the calm expert you are. Think of an architect designing an investment project for an investor. Does it make any difference to the architect whether he is designing that building for you or me or someone else? No, the architect has a job to do, designing the best investment project possible, regardless of who the client is. You should strive to be the same way. Your job is to sell the house at the best price and terms possible under the market conditions at this time. Whether you like or dislike the sellers and whether they are nice or rude to you, your job is the same. Focus on getting the job done, and work hard to keep personalities out of the picture.

PERSONAL INVOLVEMENT

Real estate salespeople have the same emotions, ambitions, drives and fears as their customers. Although we try to isolate these emotions from our job, they sometimes interfere. You should try to work toward two goals in all client relationships. The first is to separate your personal problems from your obligations to your clients. We all have problems we must cope with. The quality of life people enjoy is based on how they deal with these problems. These problems intensify and lessen in nature on a day-to-day or month-to-month or year-to-year basis, but no matter how intense our personal problems, we cannot let them interfere with the job we are doing for our customers. Our customers should not suffer because we did not make our last car payment and the bank called, looking for a check. They do not care if one of your tenants moved out in the middle of the night and trashed your best investment property. In all instances, we need to put personal problems aside and focus on the task at hand.

The second thing we need to do is to isolate our personal feelings about our customers when we handle their business. It is human nature to want to do the best job you can for your customers, but do not try to do too much. You may hurt your customers more than you help. The owner of my first listing in the real estate business was a divorced woman with financial problems and a house full of kids. I felt sorry for her and tried to sell her house for more than it was worth. This delayed a sale for months and months. We eventually reduced the house price— until we found a buyer— but to this day, I know she would have been financially and emotionally ahead if I would not have let my feelings for her situation bother me. I let my personal feelings harm my client. Try to be as proficient as possible without losing your compassion.

14

Overcoming Objections in Closing the Sale

WORKING WITH LOAN OFFICERS

Working with loan officers is an art. Most salespeople find it desirable to have a good working relationship with three to four loan officers. Two from a savings and loan and two from mortgage banks provide a good mix. Knowing a variety of loan officers from different types of institutions will help you place loans at competitive rates.

A loan officer's best work most often occurs when he or she gets full and open cooperation from the buyers and the salesperson working with the buyers. A good rule to follow is to put all the cards on the table at the time of the loan application. If you anticipate problems, it is best to explain them to the loan officer in a qualifying session before you ever show the buyers a house. This will give the loan officer an opportunity to deal with the specific challenges in getting the loan approved.

Poor Credit Report

There are some instances when bad marks on a credit report will not keep buyers from qualifying for a loan. The bad marks simply need to be addressed and explained. I had a buyer who was drafted into the army. At the time he was drafted, he had a car and a furniture payment. He couldn't sell the car or the furniture for the balances owed, so he called the credit union and furniture company and asked them for advice. They said to just sign the car and the furniture back to them. He did not realize these would show up as two foreclosures on his credit rating. When he returned from the service, he was unable to obtain credit of any type. He contacted me, said he wanted to buy a house and told me about the problem up front. I contacted a loan officer who would work with us, and we wrote up a house. Next, I made appointments with the president of the credit union and the owner of the furniture company and obtained letters from them saying the foreclosures were beyond the young man's control, and that, as far as they were concerned, he was a good risk and they would again do business with him. This did the trick.

Another credit problem that can be resolved stems from circumstances beyond the buyers' control. A catastrophic illness of a family member not covered by health insurance may cause a bad credit rating or even a forced bankruptcy. That will not necessarily keep a person from qualifying for a house. An explanatory letter from the buyers explaining the situation is usually all that is needed. The letter may make or break the buyers' case, and you would benefit from helping them compose and rewrite it to argue the necessary points as well as possible.

"Although we took this loan application, we are no longer interested in making the loan." At times, you have buyers who closely border the qualification requirements. The loan company handles the loan application and midway through the processing decide against making the loan to this party. This does not mean the loan is unattainable. Take all of the facts you have and start calling loan officers with other mortgage brokers, bankers or savings and loans in an effort to find a loan officer willing to work around the problems and repackage the loan to obtain approval.

Handling rejections by the underwriting agency.   If your loan has been packaged as well as possible and turned down by the FHA, VA, private mortgage insurers or state mortgage fund underwriters, this does not mean you will not get the loan approved. Determine exactly why the loan was refused. Whether it is ratio or credit problems, restructure the loan using the above techniques, repackage it in the best way possible and resubmit it for another consideration. If it is turned down a second time, restructure and resubmit it again. If the buyers' case was close enough to prepare the application, completing the verification problem, and completion of the loan application for underwriting, there is almost always a way the loan can be repackaged to obtain an eventual approval. This is when a really top-notch loan officer, preferably one who previously sold real estate, can go to bat and make it work. If you have buyers who want to buy and sellers who want to sell, it's almost inexcusable not to find a way to make the sale work.

WORKING WITH APPRAISERS

Obtaining a Full-Price Appraisal

The following is a marvelous technique to get the highest possible appraisal on your sales. As the listing agent, you have completed considerable market data research on the neighborhood of that house before you listed the property, when attempting to obtain adjustments and, again, when presenting an offer. You have spent as much and often more time researching the market on that particular property than the appraiser will spend in researching and completing the appraisal. In fact, if you did your job right, there is no one with a better grip on what neighboring properties are selling for than you.

With your extensive research, you are in a unique position to simultaneously aid your sellers and help the appraiser. Make photo copies of all the final sales justifying the sales price of the house, place them in an envelope, label it for the appraiser's use and either tape it to the lockbox or personally hand deliver it to the appraiser. This will accomplish two things. First, it will ensure that the appraiser will see all of the final sales, justifying the selling price. Second, it will often keep the appraiser from seeing other properties, indicating the subject property is not worth its selling price.

To ensure the best possible appraisals, always provide the appraiser with sufficient data to appraise the property at the selling price.

Handling a Low Appraisal

The following is a four-step program to deal with low appraisals.

Step number one is to ask for a formal reconsideration of the appraisal. The FHA and VA provide standard forms to ask for this reconsideration. If you truly believe the appraisal is low and can find three final sales to justify raising the appraisal, by all means ask for a reconsideration. I have a simple rule when dealing with my clients. Treat them the same way you would want to be treated by a real estate broker. If I were a seller and knew that by completing some market research and filling out a form, my agent could get my appraisal raised one, two, three or four thousand dollars, I would certainly want this to be done. Do the most complete research possible. After completing your research, type a cover letter to include with the reconsideration request form. A thoughtful, carefully reasoned letter will often persuade the appraiser to look at the property in a new light. If the reconsideration remedies the problem and produces the desired appraisal price, great. If not, you need to move on to step two.

Upon determining there is no chance of raising the appraisal price, the buyers can be approached to pay the difference in cash. This is perfectly legal and is a desirable step. If the buyers are paying more than the minimum down payment required, they may agree to the original sales price. It is helpful to explain to the buyers that the appraisal is merely a personal opinion or estimate of value. True market values are determined through negotiations between buyers and sellers. Admittedly, this is not going to work every time, but it is worth the effort if it works in even only one out of ten of the cases. As another alternative, if the buyers cannot make up the difference in cash, see if they will make up the difference in a second mortgage trust deed to the sellers.

If the buyers will not make up the difference in cash, you can often negotiate with the buyers for other concessions. You may get the buyers to complete required repairs on FHA or VA appraisals, or you may get the buyers to give the sellers some relief on costs that are legal for the buyers to pay, but that were originally to be paid by the sellers. Another possible concession is a rental adjustment if early or late occupancy is desired and/or required in the original purchase agreement.

If all of the above fail, it is time to meet with your sellers and discuss their options. In most cases, it is best for your sellers to rewrite the sale at the lower appraisal price, provided the buyers agree. There are a number of reasons for this. First, if the house sold FHA or VA, the sellers cannot request a new FHA or VA appraisal for six months. This means they cannot sell the property with this type of financing for the asking price. Even if they do find a buyer, say with FHA financing indicated rather than VA when you had a low VA appraisal, there is still a chance of getting a low FHA appraisal. Most appraisers use the same market data and appraisal principles. It is very risky to put the property on the market in hopes of obtaining a higher appraisal and finding another buyer who will pay the higher price.

If you cannot get the appraisal increased and the buyers will not make up the difference with cash or other concessions, there remain two choices for your sellers. Sell the house for less than originally agreed or put it back on the market. If they do put it back on the market, not only do they risk not finding a buyer at the higher price and getting a low appraisal, they risk losing two, three or possibly more months of carrying costs while holding the house. This can eliminate any potential gains in holding out for the original selling price.

Solving Problems on the Day of Closing

Unknown to many buyers and sellers, dozens of people must complete a job before a sale is consummated and the closing can take place. It is quite a list. Loan officers, loan processors, loan underwriters, appraisers, surveyors, termite inspectors, escrow agents, city code inspectors and insurance agents. One duty of the salespeople involved is to ensure that all involved complete their tasks in a timely fashion, so the closing will occur on schedule.

The salesperson's attitude has to be "I am getting this sale closed today no matter what!" It is your duty to carefully monitor the entire closing process from the time the purchase agreement is signed to the eventual closing to avoid and resolve delays and problems.

Unavoidably, there will still be instances when you arrive on closing day and receive a shock from the loan officer or another party that usually goes something like this: "We goofed up, somebody forgot to order the survey; I guess we are not closing today." Or, "There was a mix-up in signals, the termite inspection was not completed." When this happens, it is time for you to take charge. Do what needs to be done so the closing will take place as scheduled. Find a surveyor who can do the survey and give you a certificate that day. Find a termite inspector who will meet you before the closing and provide you with the necessary paperwork.

Going to almost any extreme to close the sale on time is worth the effort. The buyers and the sellers have been working themselves to a feverish pitch and are ready to consummate the sale. If you do not close on the scheduled day, there is a tremendous letdown for both the sellers and buyers. The sellers and buyers must be consoled with long explanations. Both parties are terribly disappointed if they cannot close on time. They not only need to be reassured but need to be psyched up for closing on another day. This is a tremendous amount of work for the salespeople involved. Not only is it a disappointment and a problem for the sellers and buyers, it is a disappointment for the agents. We do not get paid extra when sales fall apart and have to be glued back together.

One of the marks of a good salesperson is the ability to put sales back together. The mark of a better salesperson is to avoid having them fall apart in the first place. *Make every effort to get your sales closed on the scheduled closing date.*

SPECIFIC PROBLEMS ENCOUNTERED ON CLOSING DAY

The buyers have not arranged to have cash or certified funds at the closing. The broker or escrow agent who has not collected cash or certified funds at the closing cannot immediately pay the sellers. Naturally, the sellers want their proceeds as soon as the sale is closed. The best solution prior to the closing is to make absolutely sure that the buyers have talked to their banker and arranged for access to certified funds on short notice. This should be stressed when you first qualify the buyers and when the purchase agreement is written. When the purchase agreement is written, ask the buyers to check with their banker to ensure they can obtain these funds on short notice. Three or four days later or at the loan application, whichever is first, verify that the buyers have checked with their banker and have been assured they can get a certified check or cashier's check on less than a day's notice.

What if the buyers have forgotten or neglected to get their homeowner's or hazard insurance binder? This may not be apparent until you are at the closing. You should never delay a closing for such a minor problem. Go to the yellow pages and look up an insurance agent near the location of the closing. Arrange to have the insurance agent drop off a binder or pick it up, so the closing is not delayed.

The above problems are actually quite minor compared to the discovery on closing day of a significant problem with the property. Problems will range from a nonworking furnace to a previously undiscovered leaky basement to a termite infestation or damage. This is "get serious" time. It is certainly not time to delay the closing, but it is necessary to ensure that the rights of the involved parties are protected. The easiest and best way of doing this is to determine a dollar amount that will safely cover the problem. Have that much of the sellers' proceeds held in escrow, and draw up an agreement signed by the parties, stating that the problem will be corrected, paid for out of the escrow held back from the sellers' proceeds, and the sellers will receive any unused that money. This will allow you to close your sale and still make sure the last-minute problems are correctly handled.

I had an interesting last-minute title problem solved in this very way. My sellers were moving to the east coast because the husband landed a better job with a substantial increase in salary. Approximately a week before the closing, the husband notified his wife that she was not going to be moving to the east coast with him. His secretary would be joining him, and he was leaving her. Talk about distressed! Her lawyer called me the next day and said, "No matter what you do, do not close that sale." Since both the husband and wife were planning on moving out of town, albeit to two different cities, there was really no benefit in not closing the sale. At best, this would mean a delay in proceeds, and extra costs in the form of payments and utilities that would not be returned. At worst, it could generate a suit for specific performance on the part of the buyers. I suggested that the wife's lawyer get together with the husband's lawyer and write up an agreement to allow us to close the sale, deliver possession and pay everyone involved in the sale except the sellers. The sellers' proceeds would be held in our trust account until we received a court order telling us how it should be disbursed. The agreement was approved, we closed the sale, paid off the old loan company, the title company, the termite inspectors and, of course, ourselves. We had extremely pleased buyers and the best solution possible under the circumstances.

Assume that all problems on the way to the closing can be worked out, and make it so.

Index